The Christian Leaders Home Discipleship Hymnbook

Piano & Guitar Edition

Compiled and Edited by Douglas V. Horne, MMEd

Home Discipleship Press
6645 West Steger Road
Monee, IL 60449
www.homediscipleshippress.org

Acknowledgements

The editor would like to thank numerous people who have made this project possible: Kathy Wessel, Katie Boss, Lorene Franklin, Brianna Reyenga, Jerry Luedtke, Rev. Jesse Powell, Rev. Henry Reyenga, Rev. David Feddes, the congregation of Family of Faith Church, and most of all, my wife Margaret, for her continuing encouragement.

ISBN: 0-9753133-0-4

Foreword

Are traditional hymns doomed to history books?

A large number of churches and believers today sing only "contemporary" songs. While it is true that Christian music of today offers much spiritual encouragement, we should not abandon the music of our Christian heritage. Many Christians today have never experienced the rich Christian culture that traditional hymns and psalms bring to us and to our families.

Singing is an integral part of home discipleship. The Bible tells us to speak to and encourage one another with psalms, hymns, and spiritual songs. (See Col. 3:16; Eph.5:19.) For hymns and psalms to become a part of our daily lives, we need to sing and memorize them.

I want to thank Mr. Douglas Horne, Music Director for Christian Leaders, for compiling this resource specifically for home discipleship families. *The Home Discipleship Hymnbook* includes many familiar hymns and psalms that families can learn and sing. Families using *The Home Discipleship Hymnbook* will experience the reverence and beauty of our Christian worship heritage.

I suggest that each family member has his or her own hymn book. Write their names in them. After you spend time as a family reading the Bible and memorizing God's word, family members can get out their own hymnbooks to sing a hymn of the month. Sometimes you'll sing more than one song. The most important thing will be your engagement into historic and biblical worship in your own home.

My family actively practices home discipleship, including the worship of God through psalms, hymns and spiritual songs. My prayer for you is that your family will also drink abundantly from the well of traditional Christian music available in *The Home Discipleship Hymnbook.*

To learn more about home discipleship, or to find out about home discipleship churches, visit **Christian Leaders** on the web at www.Christian-leaders.org.

Sincerely,

Henry Reyenga, President
Christian Leaders

Hymn Index

A

A Child of the King .7
A Mighty Fortress Is Our God .8
A Shelter in the Time of Storm .9
Abide with Me .10
All Hail the Power of Jesus' Name .11
Am I a Soldier of the Cross? .12
Amazing Grace .13
And Can it Be? .14-15
Angels, From the Realms of Glory .16
Angels We Have Heard on High .17
As with Gladness Men of Old .18

B

Be Thou My Vision .19
Beautiful Savior .20
Beneath the Cross of Jesus .21
Blessed Assurance .22
Breathe on Me, Breath of God .23

C

Christ the Lord Is Risen Today .24
Come, Thou Almighty King .25
Crown Him with Many Crowns .26

D

Doxology (Praise God, from Whom All Blessing Flow) .80

F

Faith Is the Victory .28-29
Faith of Our Fathers .27

G

Glorious Things of Thee Are Spoken .30
God Be with You Till We Meet Again .31

H

Hallelujah, Praise Jehovah (Psalm 148) .32-33
Hallelujah, What a Savior ("Man of Sorrows," What a Name .54
Hark, the Herald Angels Sing .34
Have Thine Own Way, Lord! .35
He Leadeth Me! O Blessed Thought! .36
Holy, Holy, Holy! Lord God Almighty .37
How Firm a Foundation .38

I

I Know Not Why God's Wondrous Grace .39
I Love to Tell the Story .40
I Need Thee Every Hour .41
It Is Well (When Peace Like a River) .77

J

Jehovah Is My Light .42
Jesus, Lover of My Soul .43
Jesus Loves Me .44
Jesus Saves (We Have Heard the Joyful Sound) .72
Jesus Shall Reign Where'er the Sun .45
Joy to the World! .46
Joyful, Joyful We Adore Thee .47
Just As I Am .48

L

Leaning on the Everlasting Arms (What a Fellowship, What a Joy Divine) .73
Lead On, O King Eternal .49
Lift High the Cross .50
Like a River Glorious .51
Lord Jesus, I long to Be Perfectly Whole (Whiter Than Snow) .52
Low in the Grave He Lay .53

M

"Man of Sorrows," What a Name (Hallelujah, What a Savior) .54
My Faith Has Found a Resting Place .55
My Jesus, I Love Thee .56

N

Nearer, Still Nearer .57

O

O Come, All Ye Faithful .58
O For a Thousand Tongues to Sing .59
O Worship the King, All Glorious Above .60
Onward, Christian Soldiers .61

P

Praise God, from Whom All Blessings Flow (Doxology) .80
Praise to the Lord, the Almighty .62
Psalm 9 (Whole-hearted Thanksgiving to Thee I Will Bring) .78-79
Psalm 22 (The Ends of All the Earth Shall Hear) .68
Psalm 148 (Hallelujah, Praise Jehovah) .32-33

R

Rock of Ages, Cleft for Me .63

S

Silent Night, Holy Night .64
Stand Up, Stand Up for Jesus .65

T

Take My Life, and Let It Be .66
The Church's One Foundation .67
The Ends of All the Earth Shall Hear (Psalm 22) .68
The Solid Rock .69
This Is My Father's World .70
To God be the Glory .79

W

We Gather Together .71
We Have Heard the Joyful Sound (Jesus Saves) .72
What a Fellowship, What a Joy Divine .73
What a Friend We Have in Jesus .74
When I Survey the Wondrous Cross .75
When Morning Guilds the Skies .76
When Peace, Like A River (It Is Well) .77
Whiter than Snow (Lord Jesus, I long to Be Perfectly Whole .53
Whole-hearted Thanksgiving to Thee I Will Bring (Psalm 9) .78-79

How to Use This Book

The Home Discipleship Hymnbook is a resource designed to assist families and smaller groups with singing psalms and hymns. The format and additional resources are designed to assist you as you sing. The hymnbook itself is in a large format for easy reading, with standard arrangements of hymns for piano and optional guitar chords. Please note that the guitar chords were designed for ease of use rather than exactly matching the piano part. If you use both piano and guitar, you may want to check for incompatible chords before performing. Additional information about playing a guitar with standard hymns can be found at www.guitarhymns.com.

If you do not have a piano or guitar player in your family, you may want to obtain the optional hymn CD's. This five CD set contain piano accompaniments for all the verses of each hymn in The Home Discipleship Hymnbook. Following each hymn are individual tracks for the alto, tenor, and bass parts. The location of the CD hymn tracks for each hymn is found in a box at the bottom left corner of the corresponding hymn page.

Wind or string players will also be able to accompany your family's hymn singing by using the instrumental hymn books (release date: Fall 2004). The books are an exact transpositions of the piano parts, not a specialized arrangement.

Part Singing

A way to greatly enhance your singing is to sing in four-part harmony. This is a technique that is especially satisfying when used with older children or larger groups. Here is a brief explanation of how it works:

The standard hymns contained in this hymnal are divided into four parts; soprano, alto, tenor, and bass. The soprano part is the melody of the hymn. Most people will be able to sing this part easily. This is the part everyone sings when you are not singing in parts. When singing in parts, this pare is generally sung by the ladies. This part is not represented on the individual tracks because it is the most prominent part on the full accompaniment tracks, and thus easiest to hear. The alto line is the part directly below the soprano line on the top clef (treble clef) and is the lower female part.

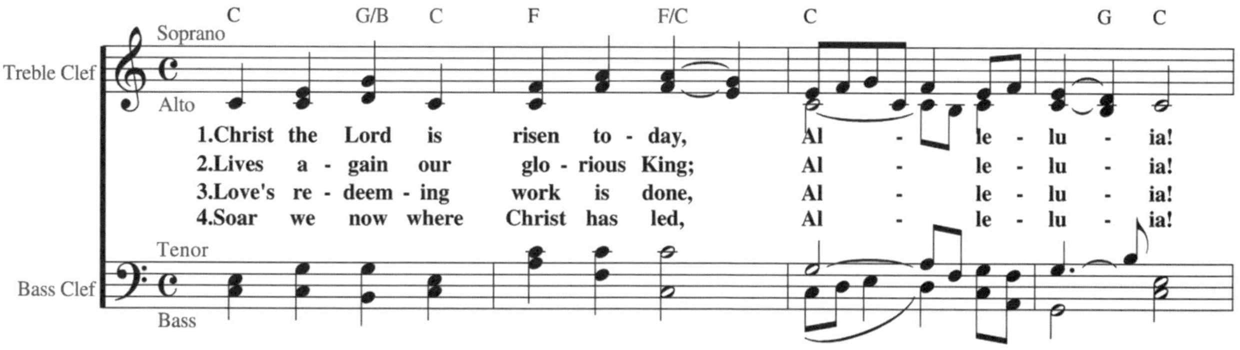
C
G/B
C
F
F/C
C
G
C
Soprano
Treble Clef
Alto
1.Christ the Lord is risen to - day, Al - le - lu - ia!
2.Lives a - gain our glo - rious King; Al - le - lu - ia!
3.Love's re - deem - ing work is done, Al - le - lu - ia!
4.Soar we now where Christ has led, Al - le - lu - ia!
Tenor
Bass Clef
Bass

The tenor line is the top notes on the bottom line of music (bass clef) and is considered the higher male part. The bass line is the lower notes in the bass clef and can, at times, get very low. Many men find that their true range is actually somewhere between the tenor and bass parts, also known as the baritone part (which does not exist in hymnals and only in specialized choral music). I recommend experimenting with either the soprano/alto parts, or the tenor/base parts, to find out which part is most comfortable to sing. Also, note that more than one part occasionally may sing the same note for several counts (as in the example, both the sopranos and altos sing the same notes on the words "Christ", "is," and "ia").

Remember, part singing is a learned skill and takes to develop in your family. I do not recommend singing parts for children under ten because their musical "ears" are still developing, and usually are not able to hear the parts.

After learning your individual part using the CD tracks or piano, the next step is to sing your part with the full accompaniment track. At first, you may find this unnerving or even impossible, and you may find yourself unconsciously switching to the melody line. Over time, and with aural repetition (I recommend you play your part over many times, using the "repeat" button on your CD player), you will find yourself better able to hear the inner voices of the hymn, and stay on pitch as you sing with the piano or piano accompaniment track.

As you develop the skill of part singing, you will find that it has a simplistic beauty of its own, especially as you get together with other families who also sing in parts, or as a church congregation. It is our hope that you will find your time of learning and singing hymns to be one of encouragement and spiritual renewal.

Another item to remember is that not all of these hymns are in four parts. Some hymns, such as "Be Thou My Vision," are designed to be sung in "unison"—which means that everyone sings the same notes.

About the editor:

Doug Horne is the Director of Music for Christian Leaders, Inc. and Family of Faith Church, Monee, IL since 2003. Prior to that, he was a music educator for over 16 years, serving in both private and public schools. Doug holds a Diploma in Bible-Theology from Moody Bible Institute, a BA in Music Education from Cedarville University, and a MMEd from Vander Cook College of Music, Chicago, IL. Doug and his wife Margaret reside in Monee, IL and have four children.

A Child of the King

Harriet E. Buell, 1834-1910

John B. Sumner, 1838-1918

Eb Bb
1. My Fa - ther is rich in hous - es and lands, He hold - eth the
2. My Fa - ther's own Son, the Sav - ior of men, Once wan - dered on
3. I once was an out - cast stran - ger on earth, A sin - ner by
Eb
wealth of the world in His hands! Of ru - bies and dia - monds, of
earth as the poor - est of them; But now He is plead - ing our
choice, and an al - ien by birth But I've been a - dopt - ed, my
Ab Eb Bb 7 Eb
sil - ver and gold, His cof - fers are full, He has rich - es un - told.
par - don on high, That we may be His when He comes by and by.
name's writ - ten down, An heir to a man - sion, a robe, and a crown.
Refrain
I'm a child of the King, A child of the King: With
Ab Eb Ab Eb Bb 7 Eb
Je - sus my Sav - ior, I'm a child of the King.

10.11.11.11. with Refrain

CD # 1 Tracks 1-4

A Mighty Fortress Is Our God

Tr. by Frederick H. Hedge, 1805-1890

Martin Luther, 1483-1546

C G Em Am D G Am Em Am Dm G7 C
1. A mighty - y for - tress is our God, A bul - wark nev - er fail - ing;
2. Did we in our own strength con - fide, Our striv - ing would be los - ing;
3. And though this world, with dev - ils filled, Should threat - en to un - do us,
4. That Word a - bove all earth - ly powers, No thanks to them, a - bid - eth;
G Em Am D G Am Em Am Dm G7 C
Our help - er He, a - mid the flood Of mor - tal ills pre - vail - ing:
Were not the right man on our side, The Man of God's own choos - ing:
We will not fear, for God hath willed His truth to tri - umph through us:
The Spir - it and the gifts are ours Through Him who with us sid - eth:
D G C F G Am E Am D7 G
For still our an - cient foe Doth seek to work us woe; His craft and power are great,
Dost ask who that may be? Christ Je - sus, it is He; Lord Sa - ba - oth His name,
The Prince of Dark - ness grim, We trem - ble not for him; His rage we can en - dure,
Let goods and kin - dred go, This mor - tal life al - so; The bod - y they may kill:
F C Dm E Am Em F C Am Dm G7 C F C
And armed with cru - el hate, On earth is not his e - qual.
From age to age the same, And He must win the bat - tle.
For lo, his doom is sure, One lit - tle Word shall fell him.
God's truth a - bid - eth still, His king - dom is for - ev - er. A - MEN.

EIN' FESTE BURG.
8. 7. 8. 7. 6. 6. 6. 6. 7.

CD # 1 Tracks 5-8

A Shelter in the Time of Storm

Vernon J. Charlesworth; adapted by Ira D. Sankey

Ira D. Sankey

F C F C7 F C
1. The Lord's our Rock, in Him we hide, A shel- ter in the time of storm;
2. A shade by day, de - fense by night, A shel - ter in the time of storm;
3. The rag - ing storms may round us beat, A shel - ter in the time of storm;
4. O Rock di - vine, O ref - uge dear, A shel - ter in the time of storm;
F C F C7 F
Se - cure what - ev - er ill be - tide, A shel - ter in the time of storm.
No fears a - larm, no foes af - fright, A shel - ter in the time of storm.
We'll nev - er leave our safe re - treat, A shel - ter in the time of storm.
Be Thou our help - er ev - er near, A shel - ter in the time of storm.
B♭ F C F C7 F
O, Je - sus is a Rock in a wea - ry land, A wea - ry land, a wea - ry land;
B♭ F C F C7 F
O, Je - sus is a Rock in a wea - ry land, A shel - ter in the time of storm.

SHELTER
L.M. with Refrain

CD # Tracks 9-12

Abide with Me

Henry F. Lyte

William H. Monk

E♭
A♭
E♭
1. A - bide with me! Fast falls the e - ven - tide.
2. Swift to its close ebbs out life's lit - tle day.
3. I need Thy pres - ence ev - 'ry pass - ing hour.
4. I fear no foe, with Thee at hand to bless;
5. Hold Thou Thy cross be - fore my clos - ing eyes;
A♭
E♭
Fm/E♭
F7/C
B♭ 7
The dark - ness deep - ens; Lord, with me a - bide!
Earth's joys grow dim; its glo - ries pass a - way.
What but Thy grace can foil the tempt - er's pow'r?
Ills have no weight, and tears no bit - ter - ness.
Shine thro' the gloom, and point me to the skies.
E♭
A♭
C7
Fm/C
When oth - er help - ers fail and com - forts flee,
Change and de - cay in all a - round I see;
Who, like Thy - self, my guide and stay can be?
Where is death's sting? Where, grave, thy vic - to - ry?
Heav'n's morn - ing breaks, and earth's vain shad - ows flee!
B♭ 7/D
E♭
A♭
E♭ /B♭
Help of the help - less, oh, a - bide with me!
O Thou who chang - est not, a - bide with me!
Thro' clouds and sun - shine, oh, a - bide with me!
I tri - umph still if Thou a - bide with me!
In life, in death, O Lord, a - bide with me! A - men.

EVENTIDE
10.10.10.10.

CD # 1 Tracks 13-16

All Hail the Power of Jesus' Name

Edward Perronet;
adapted by John Rippon

Oliver Holden

1. All hail the pow'r of Je - sus' name! Let an - gels pros - trate fall;
2. Ye cho - sen seed of Is - rael's race, Ye ran - somed from the fall,
3. Let ev - 'ry kin - dred, ev - 'ry tribe, On this ter - res - trial ball,
4. O that with yon - der sa - cred throng We at His feet may fall!
Bring forth the roy - al di - a- dem, And crown Him Lord of all;
Hail Him who saves you by His grace, And crown Him Lord of all;
To Him all maj - es - ty as- cribe, And crown Him Lord of all;
We'll join the ev - er - last- ing song, And crown Him Lord of all;
Bring forth the roy - al di- a- dem, And crown Him Lord of all!
Hail Him who saves you by His grace, And crown Him Lord of all!
To Him all maj - es - ty as- cribe, And crown Him Lord of all!
We'll join the ev - er - last- ing song, And crown Him Lord of all!

CORONATION
C.M. with Repeats

CD # 1 Tracks 17-20

Am I a Soldier of the Cross?

Issac Watts

Thomas A. Arne

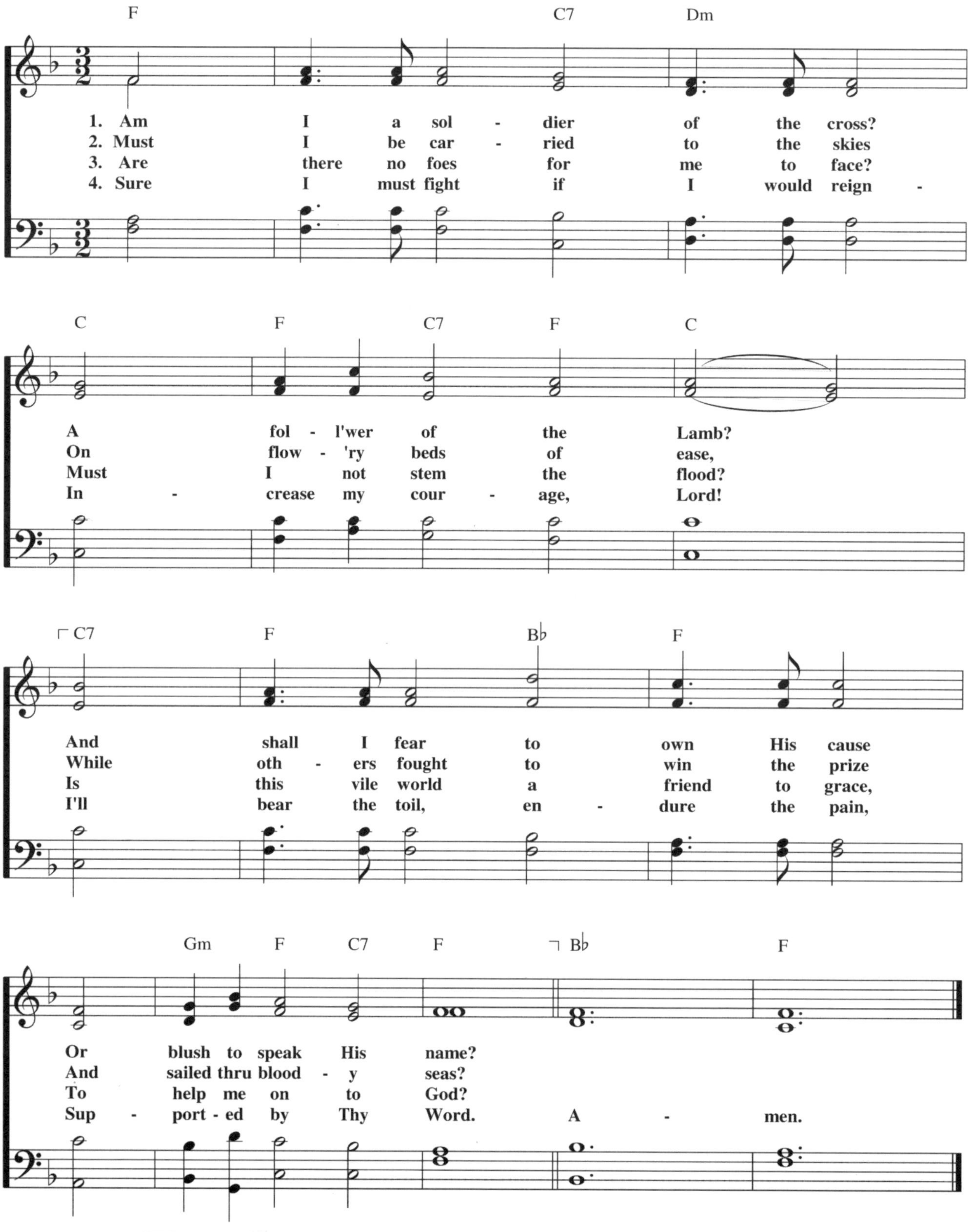
F C7 Dm
1. Am I a sol - dier of the cross?
2. Must I be car - ried to the skies
3. Are there no foes for me to face?
4. Sure I must fight if I would reign -
C F C7 F C
A fol - l'wer of the Lamb?
On flow - 'ry beds of ease,
Must I not stem the flood?
In - crease my cour - age, Lord!
C7 F B♭ F
And shall I fear to own His cause
While oth - ers fought to win the prize
Is this vile world a friend to grace,
I'll bear the toil, en - dure the pain,
Gm F C7 F B♭ F
Or blush to speak His name?
And sailed thru blood - y seas?
To help me on to God?
Sup - port - ed by Thy Word. A - men.

ARLINGTON
C.M.

CD # 1 Tracks 21-24

Amazing Grace

John Newton

Traditional American, 1831;
arr.Edwin O. Excell

G D7 Em C G
1. A - maz - ing grace! how sweet the sound, - That saved a
2. 'Twas grace that taught my heart to fear, And grace my
3. Thru man - y dan - gers, toils and snares, I have al -
4. When we've been there ten thou - sand years, Bright shin - ing
G D G C
wretch like me! I once was lost but now am
fears re - lieved; How pre - cious did that grace ap -
read - y come; 'Tis grace hath brought me safe thus
as the sun, We've no less days to sing God's
G Em G D7 G
found, Was blind but now I see.
pear The hour I first be - lieved!
far, And grace will lead me home.
praise Than when we'd first be - gun.

AMAZING GRACE
C.M.

CD # 1 Tracks 25-28

And Can It Be?

Charles Wesley

Thomas Campbell

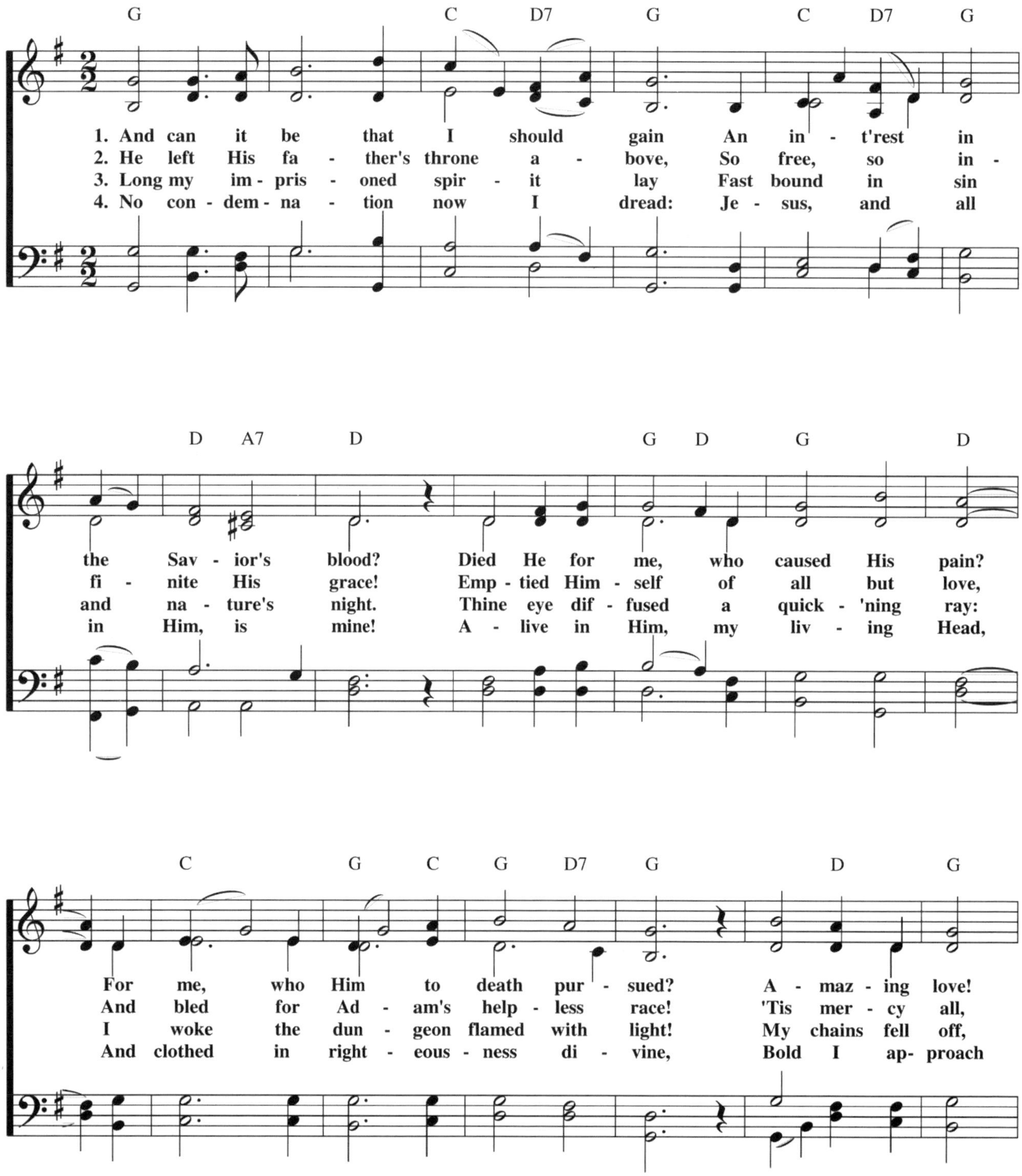
G C D7 G C D7 G
1. And can it be that I should gain An in - t'rest in
2. He left His fa - ther's throne a - bove, So free, so in -
3. Long my im - pris - oned spir - it lay Fast bound in sin
4. No con - dem - na - tion now I dread: Je - sus, and all
D A7 D G D G D
the Sav - ior's blood? Died He for me, who caused His pain?
fi - nite His grace! Emp - tied Him - self of all but love,
and na - ture's night. Thine eye dif - fused a quick - 'ning ray:
in Him, is mine! A - live in Him, my liv - ing Head,
C G C G D7 G D G
For me, who Him to death pur - sued? A - maz - ing love!
And bled for Ad - am's help - less race! 'Tis mer - cy all,
I woke the dun - geon flamed with light! My chains fell off,
And clothed in right - eous - ness di - vine, Bold I ap- proach

SAGINA
8.8.8.8.8.8. with Refrain

CD # 1 Tracks 29-32

C A7 D G
how can it be That Thou, my
im - mense and free, For, O my
my heart was free, I rose, went
th'e - ter - nal throne, And claim the
C D G
Refrain
D
God shouldst die for me?
God, it found out me.
forth, and fol - owed Thee.
crown, thru Christ my own.
A - maz - ing love! how
A - maz - ing
D7 G C G C G D7 G
can it be That Thou, my God, shouldst die for me!
love! how can it be

Angels, from the Realms of Glory

James Montgomery, 1816 | Henry T. Smart, 1867

Bb Eb Bb F7 Bb
1. An - gels, from the realms of glo - ry, Wing your flight o'er all the earth;
2. Shep - herds, in the fields a - bid - ing, Watch - ing o'er your flocks by night,
3. Sag - es, leave your con - tem - pla - tions, Bright - er vi - sions beam a - far;
4. Saints be - fore the al - ter bend - ing, Watch - ing long in hope and fear,
D7 Gm D Gm Am F C7 F
Ye who sang cre - a - tion's sto - ry, Now pro - claim Mes - si - ah's birth:
God with man is now re - sid - ing, Yon - der shines the in - fant Light:
Seek the great De - sire of na - tions, Ye have seen His na - tal star:
Sud - den - ly the Lord, de - scend - ing, In His tem - ple shall ap - pear:
F7 Bb Eb Cm G7 Cm Eb dim Cm F7 Bb
Come and wor - ship, come and wor - ship, Wor - ship Christ, the new - born King.

REGENT SQUARE
8.7.8.7.8.7.

CD # 1 Tracks 33-36

Angels We Have Heard on High

Traditional French carol

Traditional French melody

F C7 F C F
1.An - gels we have heard on high, Sweet - ly sing - ing o'er the plains,
2.Shep - herds, why this ju - bi - lee? Why your joy - ous strains pro - long?
3.Come to Beth - le - hem, and see Him whose birth the an - gels sing;
4.See with - in a man - ger laid Je - sus, Lord of heav'n and earth!
Am C7 F C F
And the moun - tains in re - ply Ech - o back their joy - ous strains.
Say what may the ti - dings be, Which in - spire your heav'n - ly song?
Come, a - dore on bend - ed knee Christ the Lord, the new - born King.
Ma - ry, Jo - seph, lend your aid, With us sing our Sav - ior's birth.
Dm Gm7 C F B♭ C C7 F C F B♭ F C7
Glo ria in ex - cel - sis De - o,
F Dm Gm7 C F B♭ C C7 F C F B♭ F C7 F
Glo ri - a in ex - cel - sis De - o.

GLORIA
7.7.7.7.Ref.

CD # 1 Tracks 37-40

As with Gladness Men of Old

William C. Dix, 1837-1898

Conrad Kocher, 1786-1872

G D7 G C D G C D G C
1. As with glad - ness men of old Did the guid - ing
2. As with joy - ous steps they sped To that low - ly
3. As they of - fered gifts most rare At that man - ger
4. Ho - ly Je - sus ev - ery day Keep us in the
G D G D G C D7 G
star be - hold; As with joy they hailed its light,
man - ger bed, There to bend the knee be - fore
rude and bare, So may we with ho - ly joy,
nar - row way; And when earth - ly things are past,
C D G C G D G D G
Lead - ing on - ward, beam - ing bright; So, most gra - cious
Him whom heaven and earth a - dore; So may we with
Pure and free from sin's al - loy, All our cost - liest
Bring our ran - somed souls at last Where they need no
D G C D G C G D7 G
Lord, may we Ev - er - more be led to Thee.
will - ing feet Ev - er seek Thy mer - cy seat.
treas - ures bring, Christ, to Thee, our heaven - ly King.
star to guide, Where no clouds Thy glo - ry hide.

DIX
7.7.7.7.7.7.

CD # 1 Tracks 41-44

Be Thou My Vision

Ancient Irish,
Tr. by Mary E. Byrne, 1927,
Versified by Eleanor H. Hull, 1927

Traditional Irish Melody,
Harmonized by David Evans, 1927

E♭ B♭ A♭ E♭
Unison
1.Be Thou my Vi - sion, O Lord of my heart;
2.Be Thou my Wis - dom, and Thou my true Word;
3.Rich - es I heed not, nor man's emp - ty praise,
4.High King of heav - en, my vic - to - ry won,
B♭ Cm7 A♭ B♭
Naught be all else to me, save that Thou art
I ev - er with Thee and Thou with me, Lord;
Thou mine in - her - i - tance, now and al - ways;
May I reach heav - ens joys, O bright heav'ns Sun!
Cm7 E♭ A♭ B♭
Thou my best thought, by day or by night,
Thou my great Fa - ther, I Thy true son;
Thou and Thou on - ly, first in my heart,
Heart of my own heart, what - ev - er be - fall,
Cm B♭ E♭ A♭ E♭
Wak - ing or sleep - ing Thy pres - ence my light.
Thou in me dwell - ing, and I with Thee one.
High King of heav - en, my Treas - ure Thou art.
Still be my Vi - sion, O Rul - er of all. A - men.

SLANE
10.10.9.10.

CD # 1 Tracks 45

Beautiful Savior

Author unknown, 1677
Tr., Joseph A. Seiss, 1873

"Schlesische Volkslieder," Leipzig, 1842

1. Beau - ti - ful Sav - ior, King of Cre - a - tion, Son of
2. Fair are the mead - ows, Fair are the wood - lands, Robed in
3. Fair is the sun - shine, Fair is the moon - light, Bright the
4. Beau - ti - ful Sav - ior, Lord of the na - tions, Son of
God and Son of Man! Tru - ly I'd love Thee, Tru - ly I'd
flow'rs of bloom - ing spring; Je - sus is fair - er, Je - sus is
spar - kling stars on high; Je - sus shines bright - er, Je - sus shines
God and Son of Man! Glo - ry and hon - or, Praise, ad - o -
serve Thee, Light of my soul, my Joy, my Crown.
pur - er; He makes our sor - r'wing spir - it sing.
pur - er, Than all the an - gels in the sky.
ra - tion, Now and for - ev - er - more be Thine! A - men.

CRUSADER'S HYMN
5.5.7.5.5.8.

CD # 1 Tracks 46-49

Beneath the Cross of Jesus

Elizabeth C. Clephane, 1830-1869 | Frederick C. Maker, 1844-1927

C G7 C
1. Be - neath the cross of Je - sus I fain would take my stand,
2. Up - on that cross of Je - sus Mine eye at times can see
3. I take, O Cross, thy shad - ow For my a - bid - ing place;
Am G B A Dm Am F E
The shad - ow of a might - y rock With - in a wear - y land;
The ver - y dy - ing form of One Who suf - fered there for me;
I ask no oth - er sun - shine than The sun - shine of His face;
Am F A Dm
A home with - in the wil - der - ness, A rest up - on the way,
And from my smit - ten heart with tears Two won - ders I con - fess,
Con - tent to let the world go by, To know no gain or loss,
G7 C F C G7 C
From the burn - ing of the noon - tide heat And the bur - den of the day.
The won - ders of His glo - rious love And my un - wor - thi - ness.
My sin - ful self my on - ly shame, My glo - ry all the cross.

ST. CHRISTOPHER
7.6.8.6.8.6.8.6.

CD # 1 Tracks 50-53

Blessed Assurance

Fanny J. Crosby, 1873

Phoebe P. Knapp, 1873

D G D A E
1.Bless - ed as - sur - ance, Je - sus is mine! O what a fore - taste of glo - ry di -
2.Per - fect sub - mis - sion, per - fect de - light, Vi - sions of rap - ture now burst on my
3.Per - fect sub - mis - sion, all is at rest, I in my Sav - ior am hap - py and
A D G D
vine! Heir of sal - va - tion, pur - chase of God, Born of His
sight; An - gels de - scend - ing, bring from a - bove Ech - oes of
blest; Watch - ing and wait - ing look - ing a - bove, Filled with His
G A A7 D Refrain G
Spir - it, washed in His blood.
mer - cy, whis - pers of love. This is my sto - ry, this is my
good - ness, lost in His love.
D G D A E A
song, Prais - ing my Sav - ior all the day long; This is my
D G D G Em A7 D
sto - ry this is my song, Prais - ing my Sav - ior all the day long.

ASSURANCE
9.10.9.9.Ref.

CD # 1 Tracks 54-57

Breathe on Me, Breath of God

Edwin Hatch, 1835-1889 | Robert Jackson, 1842-1914

F Bb F Dm C F
1. Breathe on me, Breath of God, Fill me with life a -
2. Breathe on me, Breath of God, Un - til my heart is
3. Breathe on me, Breath of God, Till I am whol - ly
4. Breathe on me, Breath of God, So shall I nev - er
C F C Dm Bb
new, That I may love what Thou dost love, And
pure, Un - til with Thee I will Thy will, To
Thine, Till all this earth - ly part of me Glows
die, But live with Thee the per - fect life Of
F C F Bb F
do what Thou wouldst do.
do and to en - dure.
with Thy fire di - vine.
Thine e - ter - ni - ty.
A - MEN.

TRENTHAM
S.M.

CD # 1 Tracks 58-61

Christ the Lord Is Risen Today

Charles Wesley, 1739

Arr. from Lyra Davidica,
London, 1708

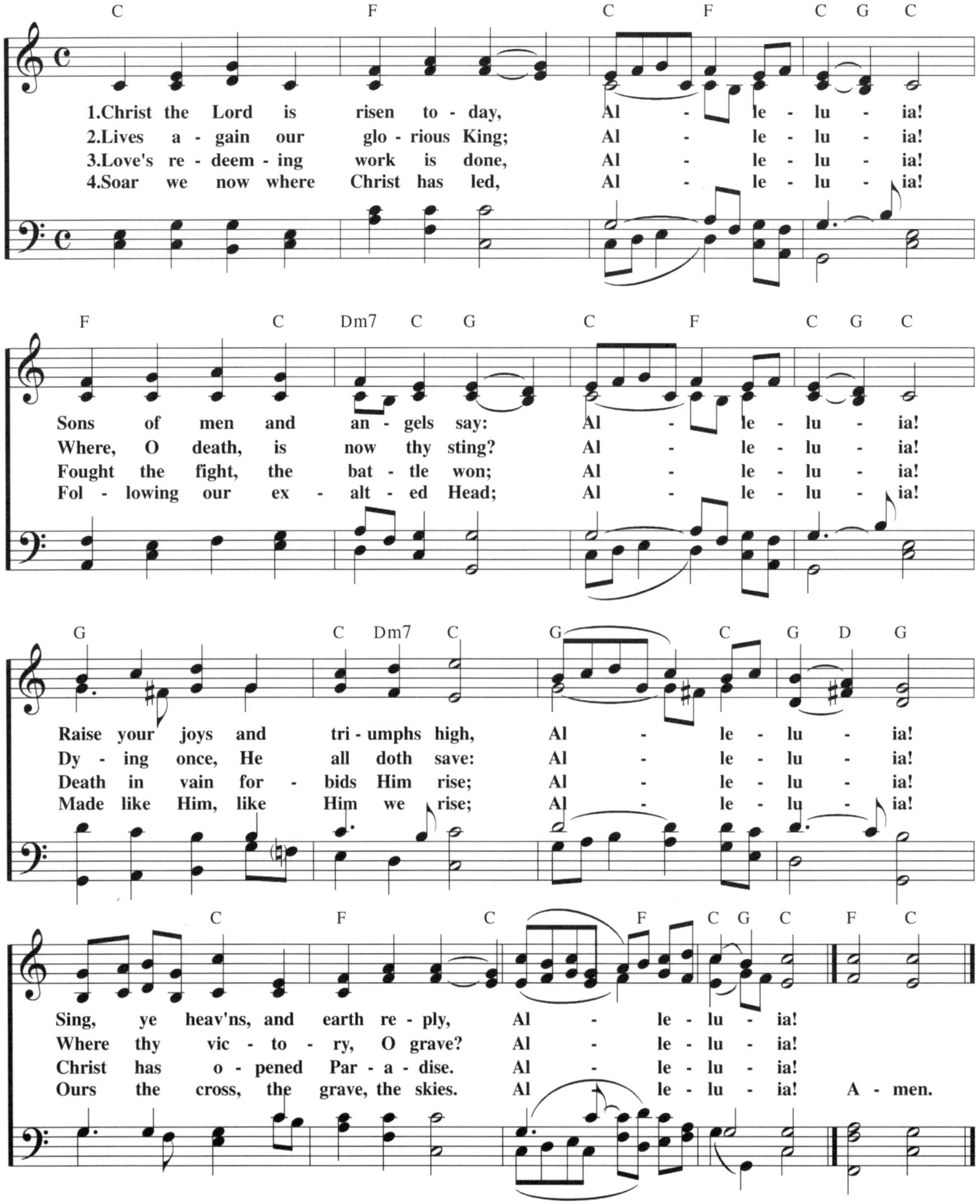
C F C F C G C
1.Christ the Lord is risen to - day, Al - le - lu - ia!
2.Lives a - gain our glo - rious King; Al - le - lu - ia!
3.Love's re - deem - ing work is done, Al - le - lu - ia!
4.Soar we now where Christ has led, Al - le - lu - ia!
F C Dm7 C G C F C G C
Sons of men and an - gels say: Al - le - lu - ia!
Where, O death, is now thy sting? Al - le - lu - ia!
Fought the fight, the bat - tle won; Al - le - lu - ia!
Fol - lowing our ex - alt - ed Head; Al - le - lu - ia!
G C Dm7 C G C G D G
Raise your joys and tri - umphs high, Al - le - lu - ia!
Dy - ing once, He all doth save: Al - le - lu - ia!
Death in vain for - bids Him rise; Al - le - lu - ia!
Made like Him, like Him we rise; Al - le - lu - ia!
C F C F C G C F C
Sing, ye heav'ns, and earth re - ply, Al - le - lu - ia!
Where thy vic - to - ry, O grave? Al - le - lu - ia!
Christ has o - pened Par - a - dise. Al - le - lu - ia!
Ours the cross, the grave, the skies. Al - le - lu - ia! A - men.

EASTER HYMN
7.7.7.7. Alleluias

CD # 1 Tracks 62-65

Come, Thou Almighty King

Anonymous

Felice de Giardini, 1716-1796

F Gm C F C F B♭ F C
1. Come, Thou Al - might - y King, Help us Thy name to sing,
2. Come, Thou In - car- nate Word, Gird on Thy might - y sword,
3. Come, Ho - ly Com - fort - er, Thy sa - cred - wit - ness bear,
4. To Thee, great One in Three, E - ter - nal prais - es be,
F C F C C7 F
Help us to praise: Fa - ther, all - glo - ri – ous, O'er all vic - to - ri - ous,
Scat - ter Thy foes. Let Thine al - might - y aid Our sure de - fense be made,
In this glad hour! Thou, who al - might – y art, Rule now in ev - 'ry heart,
Hence ev - er - more; Thy sov - 'reign maj - es - ty May we in glo - ry see,
F B♭ F B♭ F C7 F B♭ F
Come, and reign o - ver us, An - cient of Days.
Our souls on Thee be stayed; Thy won - ders show.
And ne'er from us de - part, Spir - it of pow'r.
And to e - ter - ni - ty Love and a - dore.
A - MEN.

ITALIAN HYMN (Trinity)
6.6.4.6.6.6.4.

CD # 2 Tracks 1-4

Crown Him with Many Crowns

Matthew Bridges, 1851, and
Godfrey Thring, 1874

George J. Elvey, 1816-1893

D G D G D A
1. Crown Him with man - y crowns, The Lamb up - on His throne;
2. Crown Him the Lord of life, Who tri - umphed o'er the grave,
3. Crown Him the Lord of peace, Whose power a scep - ter sways
4. Crown Him the Lord of love; Be - hold His hands and side,
D G D E A D A E7 A
Hark! how the heaven - ly an - them drowns All mu - sic but its own:
And rose vic - to - rious in the strife For those He came to save;
From pole to pole, that wars may cease, And all be prayer and praise:
Those wounds, yet vis - i - ble a - bove, In beau - ty glo - ri - fied:
D G E A
A - wake, my soul, and sing Of Him who died for thee,
His glo - ries now we sing Who died, and rose on high,
His reign shall know no end, And round His pierc - ed feet
All hail, Re - deem - er, hail! For Thou hast died for me:
A D G D Em7 A D G A A7 D G D
And hail Him as thy match-less King Through all e - ter - ni - ty.
Who died e - ter-nal life to bring, And lives that death may die.
Fair flowers of par-a- dise ex - tend Their fra-grance ev - er sweet.
Thy praise and glo-ry shall not fail Through - out e - ter - ni - ty. A - MEN.

DIADEMATA
S. M. D.

CD # 2 Tracks 5-8

Faith of Our Fathers

Frederick W. Faber

Henry F. Hemy; arranged by James G. Walton

G Am D7 G C G
1. Faith of our fa - thers! liv - ing still In spite of dun - geon,
2. Our fa - thers, chained in pris - ons dark, Were still in heart and
3. Faith of our fa - thers! we will love Both friend and foe in
A7 D G Am D7 G
fire and sword: O how our hearts beat high with joy
con - science free: How sure will be their chil - dren's peace
all our strife: And preach thee too as love knows how,
C G Em7 A7 D7 G C G
When-e'er we hear that glo - rious word! Faith of our fa - thers,
If they like them con - tend - for thee! Faith of our fa - thers,
By kind - ly words and vir - tuous life: Faith of our fa - thers,
D G C Em D D7 G
ho - ly faith! We will be true to thee till death!
ho - ly faith! We will be true to thee till death!
ho - ly faith! We will be true to thee till death!

ST. CATHERINE
8.8.8.8.8.8.

CD # 2 Tracks 13-16

Faith Is the Victory

John H. Yates

Ira D. Sankey

Eb Bb 7 Eb
1. En - camped a - long the hills of light, Ye Chris - tian sol - diers, rise,
2. His ban - ner o - ver us is love, Our sword the Word of God;
3. On ev - ery hand the foe we find Drawn up in dread ar - ray;
4. To him that o - ver - comes the foe, White rai - ment shall be giv'n;
Bb 7 Eb
And press the bat - tle e're the night Shall veil the glow - ing skies.
We tread the road the saints a - bove With shouts of tri - umph trod.
Let tents of ease be left be - hind, And on - ward to the fray;
Be - fore the an - gels he shall know His name con - fessed in heav'n.
Bb 7 Eb Bb 7 F Bb 7
A - gainst the foe in vales be - low Let all our strength be hurled;
By faith they, like a whirl-wind's breath, Swept on o'er ev - 'ry field;
Sal - va - tion's hel - met on each head, With truth all girt a - bout,
Then on - ward from the hills of light, Our hearts with love a - flame,
Eb Bb 7 Ab Eb Bb 7 Eb
Faith is the vic - to - ry, we know, That o - ver - comes the world.
The faith by which they con - quered death Is still our shin - ing shield.
The earth shall trem - ble 'neath our tread, And ech - o with our shout.
We'll van - quish all the hosts of night, In Je - sus' con - quering name.

SANKEY
C.M.D. with Refrain

CD # 2 Tracks 9-12

Refrain
B♭7 A♭ E♭
Faith is the vic - to - ry! Faith is the vic - to - ry!
A♭ E♭ B♭7 E♭
O, glo - ri - ous vic - to - ry, That o - ver - comes the world.

Glorious Things of Thee Are Spoken

John Newton, 1725-1807 Francis J. Haydn, 1732-1809

F C F C Gm F C F Dm Am Gm F Gm F C
1. Glo - rious things of thee are spo - ken, Zi - on cit - y of our God;
2. See, the streams of liv - ing wa - ters, Spring - ing from e - ter - nal Love,
3. Round each hab - i - ta - tion hov-- ering, See the cloud and fire ap - pear
4. Sav - ior, if of Zi - on's cit - y I, through grace, a mem - ber am,
F C F C Gm F C F Dm Am Gm F Gm F C
He, whose word can - not be bro - ken, Formed thee for His own a - bode:
Well sup - ply thy sons and daugh - ters, And all fear of want re - move:
For a glo - ry and a cov - ering, Show - ing that the Lord is near!
Let the world de - ride or pit - y, I will glo - ry in Thy Name.
F C Bb F C Gm F G C
On the Rock of A - ges found - ed, What can shake thy sure re - pose?
Who can faint, while such a riv - er Ev - er flows their thirst t'as - suage?
Glo - rious things of thee are spo - ken, Zi - on, cit - y of our God;
Fad - ing is the world - ling's pleas - ure, All His boast - ed pomp and show;
F Dm F Bb F C F C Am F Bb F C F Bb F
With sal - va - tion's walls sur - round - ed, Thou may'st smile at all thy foes.
Grace which, like the Lord, the Giv - er, Nev - er fails from age to age.
He, whose word can - not be bro - ken, Formed thee for His own a - bode.
Sol - id joys and last - ing treas - ure None but Zi - on's chil - dren know. A - MEN.

AUSTRIAN HYMN
8.7.8.7.D.

CD # 2 Tracks 17-20

God Be with You Till We Meet Again

Jeremiah E. Rankin, 1880 | William G. Tomer, 1880

C G C F C
1.God be with you till we meet a-gain; By His coun-sels guide,-up-hold you,
2.God be with you till we meet a-gain, 'Neath His wings pro-tect-ing hide you,
3.God be with you till we meet a-gain; When life's per-ils thick con-found you,
4.God be with you till we meet a-gain; Keep love's ban-ner float-ing o'er you,
G C G7 C
Refrain
With His sheep se-cure-ly fold you; God be with you till we meet a-gain.
Dai-ly man-na still pro-vide you; God be with you till we meet a-gain. Till we
Put His arms un-fail-ing round you; God be with you till we meet a-gain.
Smite death's threat' ning wave be-fore you; God be with you till we meet a-gain.
F C G C
meet, till we meet, Till we meet at Je-sus' feet; Till we
Till we meet, till we meet, till we meet, till we meet,
F C G7 C
meet, till we meet, God be with you till we meet a-gain.
Till we meet, till we meet, till we meet,

GOD BE WITH YOU
Irreg.

CD # 2 Tracks 21-24

Hallelujah, Praise Jehovah

Psalm 148

William J. Kirkpatrick, 1838-1921

G
1.Hal - le - lu - jah, praise Je - ho - vah, From the heav - ens praise His
2.Let them prais - es give Je - ho - vah, They were made at His com -
3.All ye fruit - ful trees and ce - dars, All ye hills and moun - tains
D G D Bm
Name; Praise Je - ho - vah in the high - est, All His an - gels, praise pro -
mand; Them for - ev - er He es - tab - lished, His de - cree shall ev - er
high, Creep - ing things and beasts and cat - tle, Birds that in the heav - ens
D Am D D7
claim. All His hosts, to - geth - er praise Him, Sun and moon and stars on
stand. From the earth, O praise Je - ho - vah, All ye seas, ye mon - sters
fly, Kings of earth, and all ye peo - ple, Prin - ces great, earth's judg - es
D G D G Am G D7 G
high; Praise Him, O ye heavens of heav - ens, And ye floods a - bove the sky.
all, Fire and hail and snow and va - pors, Storm - y winds that hear His call.
all; Praise His Name, young men and maid - ens, A - ged men, and chil - dren small.

KIRKPATRICK
8.7.8.7.D.with Refrain

CD # 2 Tracks 25-28

Refrain
G
Let them prais - es give Je - ho - vah, For His
Let them prais - es
C D G
Name a - lone is high, And His glo - ry is ex -
And His glo - ry
alt - ed And His glo - ry is ex - alt - ed, And His
And His glo - ry
C G D D7 G
glo - ry is ex - alt - ed, Far a - bove the earth and sky.
And His glo - ry

Hark, the Herald Angels Sing

TEXT: Charles Wesley, 1739

Felix Mendelssohn-Bartholdy, 1840
Arr. by William H. Cummings, 1856

F C F B♭ F C F
1. Hark, the her - ald an - gels sing, "Glo - ry to the new - born King,
2. Christ, by high - est heav'n a - dored, Christ, the ev - er - last - ing Lord:
3. Hail the heav'n - born Prince of Peace! Hail the Sun of right - eous - ness!
Dm G7 C G7 C
Peace on earth, and mer - cy mild; God and sin - ners rec - on - ciled!"
Late in time be - hold Him come, Off - spring of the Vir - gin's womb.
Light and life to all He brings, Ris'n with heal - ing in His wings:
B♭ F C F B♭ F C
Joy - ful, all ye na - tions, rise, Join the tri - umph of the skies;
Veiled in flesh the God - head see, Hail the in - car - nate De - i - ty!
Mild He lays His glo - ry by, Born that man no more may die;
B♭ Gm D7 Gm7 C F C F
With the an - gel - ic hosts pro - claim, "Christ is born in Beth - le - hem."
Pleased as man with men to dwell, Je - sus, our Em - man - u - el.
Born to raise the sons of earth; Born to give them sec - ond birth.
B♭ Gm D7 Gm7 C F C F
Hark, the her - ald an - gels sing, "Glo - ry to the new - born King!"
Hark, the her - ald an - gels sing, "Glo - ry to the new - born King!"
Hark, the her - ald an - gels sing, "Glo - ry to the new - born King!"

MENDELSSOHN
7. 7. 7. 7. D. with Refrain

CD # 2 Tracks 29-32

Have Thine Own Way, Lord!

Adelaide A. Pollard, 1906

George C. Stebbins, 1907

E♭ A♭ E♭ B♭7
1. Have Thine own way, Lord! Have Thine own way! Thou art the
2. Have Thine own way, Lord! Have Thine own way! Search me and
3. Have Thine own way, Lord! Have Thine own way! Wound - ed and
4. Have Thine own way, Lord! Have Thine own way! Hold o'er my
B♭ E♭ A♭ E♭
Pot - ter; I am the clay Mould me and make me Aft - er Thy
try me, Mas - ter, to - day! O - pen mine eyes, my sin show me
wea - ry, Help me, I pray! Pow - er all pow - er Sure - ly is
be - ing Ab - so - lute sway! Fill with Thy Spir - it Till all shall
A♭ E♭ B♭7 E♭
will, While I am wait - ing, Yield - ed and still.
now, As in Thy pres - ence Hum - bly I bow.
Thine! Touch me and heal me, Sav - ior di - vine!
see Christ on - ly, al - ways, Liv - ing in me!

ADELAIDE
5. 4. 5. 4. D.

CD # 2 Tracks 33-36

He Leadeth Me! O Blessed Thought!

Joseph H. Gilmore, 1862

William B. Bradbury, 1864

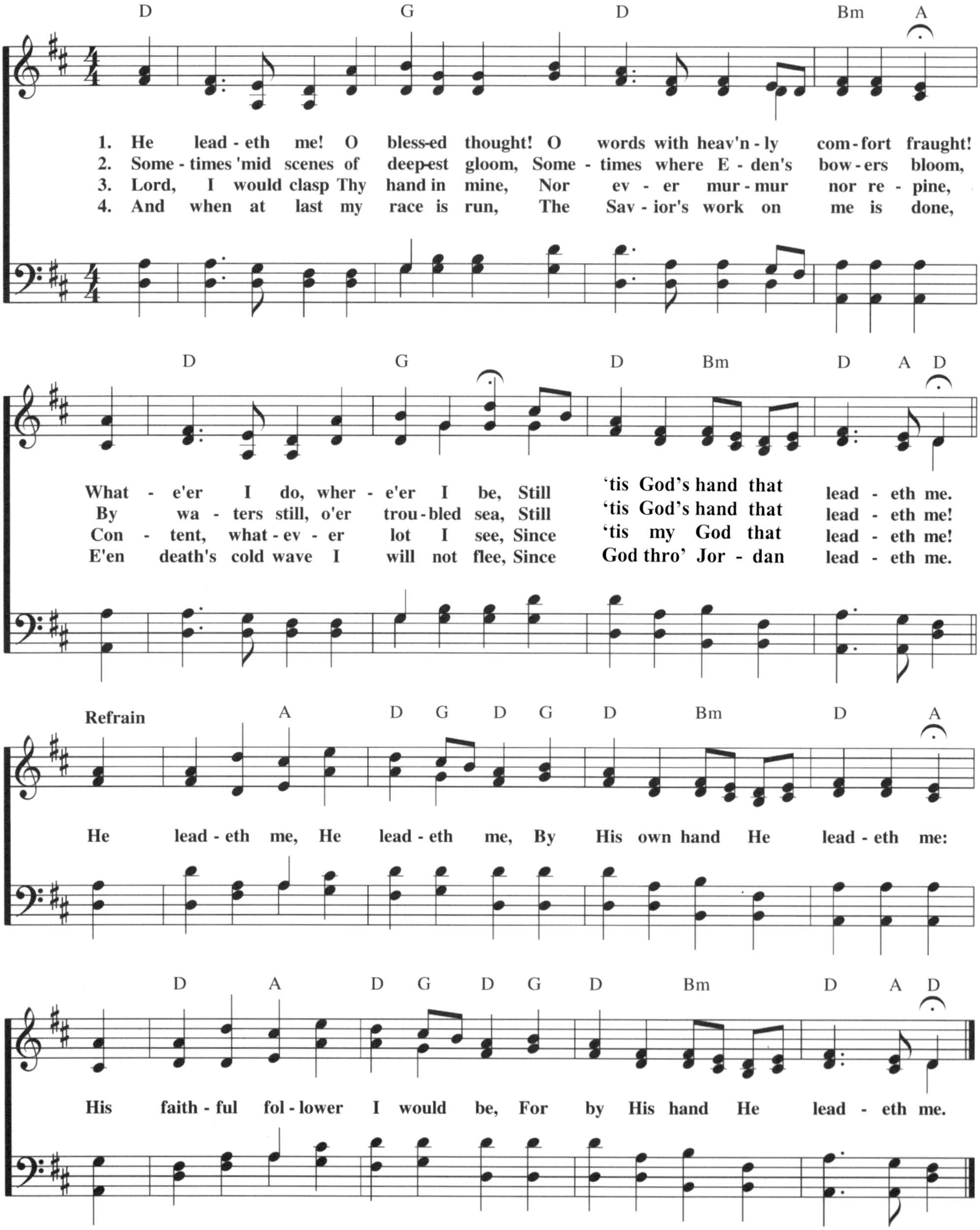
D G D Bm A
1. He lead - eth me! O bless-ed thought! O words with heav'n - ly com - fort fraught!
2. Some - times 'mid scenes of deep-est gloom, Some - times where E - den's bow - ers bloom,
3. Lord, I would clasp Thy hand in mine, Nor ev - er mur - mur nor re - pine,
4. And when at last my race is run, The Sav - ior's work on me is done,
D G D Bm D A D
What - e'er I do, wher - e'er I be, Still 'tis God's hand that lead - eth me.
By wa - ters still, o'er trou - bled sea, Still 'tis God's hand that lead - eth me!
Con - tent, what - ev - er lot I see, Since 'tis my God that lead - eth me!
E'en death's cold wave I will not flee, Since God thro' Jor - dan lead - eth me.
Refrain
A D G D G D Bm D A
He lead - eth me, He lead - eth me, By His own hand He lead - eth me:
D A D G D G D Bm D A D
His faith - ful fol - lower I would be, For by His hand He lead - eth me.

HE LEADETH ME
L. M. with refrain

CD # 2 Tracks 37-40

Holy, Holy, Holy! Lord God Almighty

Reginald Heber, 1826

John B. Dykes, 1861

D Bm A G D
1. Ho - ly, ho - ly, ho - ly! Lord God Al - might - y!
2. Ho - ly, ho - ly, ho - ly! All the saints a - dore Thee,
3. Ho - ly, ho - ly, ho - ly! Though the dark - ness hide thee,
4. Ho - ly, ho - ly, ho - ly! Lord God Al - might - y!
A Bm A E7 A
Ear - ly in the morn - ing our song shall rise to Thee.
cast - ing down their gold - en crowns a - round the glass - y sea;
though the eye of sin - ful man thy glo - ry may not see,
All Thy works shall praise Thy name, in earth and sky and sea.
D Bm A G D
Ho - ly, ho - ly, ho - ly! Mer - ci - ful and might - y,
cher - u - bim and ser - a - phim fall - ing down be - fore Thee,
on - ly Thou art ho - ly; there is none be - side Thee,
Ho - ly, ho - ly, ho - ly! Mer - ci - ful and might - y,
Bm D G D G A7 D
God in Three Per - sons, bless - ed Trin - i - ty!
Who wert, and art, and ev - er - more shalt be.
per - fect in power, in love and pur - i - ty.
God in Three Per - sons, bless - ed Trin - i - ty.

NICAEA
11. 12. 12. 10

CD # 2 Tracks 41-44

How Firm a Foundation

"K" in Rippon's Selection, 1787

Early American Melody

G C G Em D
1. How firm a foun - da - tion, ye saints of the Lord,
2. "Fear not, I am with thee; O be not dis - mayed,
3. "When through fier - y tri - als thy path - way shall lie,
4. "The soul that on Je - sus hath leaned for re - pose
G C G Em G D G
Is laid for your faith in His ex - cel - lent Word!
For I am thy God, and will still give thee aid;
My grace, all - suf - fi - cient, shall be thy sup - ply:
I will not, I will not de - sert to his foes;
Em C G Em D
What more can He say than to you He hath said,
I'll strength - en thee, help thee, and cause thee to stand,
The flame shall not hurt thee; I on - ly de - sign
That soul, though all hell should en - deav - or to shake,
G C G Em G D G C G
To you who for ref - uge to Je - sus have fled?
Up - held by my right - eous, om - nip - o - tent hand.
Thy dross to con - sume, and thy gold to re - fine.
I'll nev - er, no, nev - er, no, nev - er for - sake!" A - MEN.

FOUNDATION
11. 11. 11. 11.

CD # 2 Tracks 45-48

I Know Not Why God's Wondrous Grace

Daniel W. Whittle, 1840-1901

James McGranahan, 1840-1907

E♭ A♭ E♭
1.I know not why God's won - drous grace To me He hath made
2.I know not how this sav - ing faith To me He did im -
3.I know not how the Spir - it moves, Con - vinc - ing men of
4.I know not what of good or ill May be re - served for
B♭7 E♭ A♭ B♭7
known, Nor why, un - wor - thy, Christ in love Re - deemed me for His
part, Nor how be - liev - ing in His Word Wrought peace with - in my
sin, Re - veal - ing Je - sus through the Word, Cre - at - ing faith in
me, Of wea - ry ways or gold - en days, Be - fore His face I
E♭ A♭ E♭ B♭7
own.
heart. But "I know whom I have be - liev - ed, and am per - suad - ed that He is
Him.
see.
E♭ A♭ E♭ B♭7 E♭
a - ble To keep that which I've com - mit - ted Un - to Him a - gainst that day."

EL NATHAN
C.M., Ref.

CD # 2 Tracks 49-52

I Love to Tell the Story

A. Catherine Hankey

William G. Fischer

1. I love to tell the sto - ry of un - seen things a - bove, Of Je - sus
2. I love to tell the sto - ry; 'Tis pleas - ant to re - peat What seems, each
3. I love to tell the sto - ry, for those who know it best Seem hun - ger -
and His glo - ry, of Je - sus and His love; I love to tell the
time I tell it, more won - der - ful - ly sweet; I love to tell the
ing and thirst - ing to hear it like the rest; And when in scenes of
sto - ry be - cause I know 'tis true, It sat - is - fies my long - ings
sto - ry, for some have nev - er heard The mes - sage of sal - va - tion
glo - ry I sing the new, new song, 'Twill be the old, old sto - ry
as noth - ing else can do.
from God's own ho - ly Word.
that I have loved so long.
Refrain
I love to tell the sto - ry! 'Twill be my
theme in glo - ry To tell the old, old sto - ry Of Je - sus and His love.

HANKEY
7.6.7.6.D. with Refrain

CD # 2 Tracks 53-56

I Need Thee Every Hour

Annie S. Hawks; Robert Lowry, Refrain

Robert Lowry

G C G
1. I need Thee ev - 'ry hour, Most gra - cious Lord;
2. I need Thee ev - 'ry hour, Stay Thou near - by;
3. I need Thee ev - 'ry hour, In joy or pain;
4. I need Thee ev - 'ry hour, Teach me Thy will,
5. I need Thee ev - 'ry hour, Most Ho - ly One;
D G D A D
No ten - der voice like Thine Can peace af - ford.
Temp - ta - tions lose their pow'r When Thou art nigh.
Come quick - ly, and a - bide, Or life is vain.
And Thy rich prom - is - es In me ful - fill.
O make me Thine in - deed, Thou bless - ed Son!
Refrain
G C G D D7 G
I need Thee, O I need Thee; Ev - 'ry hour I need Thee!
C G C G D7 G
O bless me now, my Sav - ior, I come to Thee.

NEED
6.4.6.4. with Refrain

CD # 2 Tracks 57-60

Jehovah Is My Light

PSALM 27

English, 1826

A♭ D♭
1.Je - ho - vah is my light, And my sal - va - tion
2.When e - vil - do - ers came To make my life their
3.My one re - quest has been, And still this prayer I
4.When trou - bles round me swell, When fears and dan - gers
5.Up - lift - ed on a rock A - bove my foes a -
A♭ E♭
near; Who shall my soul af - fright, Or cause my heart to
prey, They stum - bled in their shame And fell in sore dis -
raise, - That I may dwell with - in God's house through all my
throng, Se - cure - ly I will dwell In His pa - vil - ion
round, A - mid the bat - tle shock My song shall still re -
E♭7 A♭ E♭7
fear? While God my strength, my life sus -
may; Though hosts make war on ev - ery
days, Je - ho - vah's beau - ty to ad -
strong; With - in the co - vert of His
sound; Then joy - ful of - ferings I will
A♭ D♭ Fmin A♭ E♭7 A♭
stains, Se - cure from fear my soul re - mains.
side, Still fear - less I in God con - fide.
mire, And in His tem - ple to in - quire.
tent He hides me till the storm is spent.
bring, Je - ho - vah's praise my heart shall sing.

MILLENNIUM
6.6.6.6.8.8.

CD # 3 Tracks 1-4

Jesus, Lover of My Soul

Charles Wesley, 1707-1788

Simeon B. Marsh, 1798-1875

1. Je - sus, Lov - er of my soul, Let me to Thy bos - om fly,
2. Oth - er ref - uge have I none; Hangs my help - less soul on Thee;
3. Thou, O Christ, art all I want; More than all in Thee I find:
4. Plen - teous grace with Thee is found, Grace to cov - er all my sin;
While the near - er wa - ters roll, While the tem - pest still is high:
Leave, O leave me not a - lone, Still sup - port and com - fort me:
Raise the fall - en, cheer the faint, Heal the sick, and lead the blind.
Let the heal - ing streams a - bound; Make and keep me pure with - in.
Hide me, O my Sav - iour, hide, Till the storm of life is past;
All my trust on Thee is stayed, All my help from Thee I bring;
Just and ho - ly is Thy Name, I am all un - right - eous - ness;
Thou of life the Foun - tain art, Free - ly let me take of Thee:
Safe in - to the ha - ven guide; O re - ceive my soul at last!
Cov - er my de - fense - less head With the shad - ow of Thy wing.
False and full of sin I am, Thou art full of truth and grace.
Spring Thou up with - in my heart, Rise to all e - ter - ni - ty. A - men.

MARTYN (First Tune)
7.7.7.7.D.

CD # 3 Tracks 5-8

Jesus Loves Me

Anna B. Warner, 1860

William B. Bradbury, 1862

C F C
1. Je - sus loves me! This I know, for the Bi - ble tells me so.
2. Je - sus loves me! He who died Heav - en's gate to o - pen wide;
3. Je - sus loves me! He will stay Close be - side me all the way;
4. Je - sus loves me! still to - day, walk - ing with me on my way.
F C G7 C
Lit - tle ones to him be - long; they are weak, but he is strong.
He will wash a - way my sin, Let His lit - tle child come in.
Thou hast bled and died for me, I will hence - forth live for Thee.
Want - ing as a friend to give light and love to all who live.
F C G7
Yes, Je - sus loves me! Yes, Je - sus loves me!
C F C G7 C
Yes, Je - sus loves me! The Bi - ble tells me so.
8

German

Jesus liebt mich ganz gewiss,
Denn die Bible sagt mir dies,
All Kinder schwach und klein,
Lad't Er herzlich zu sich ein.
Ja, Jesus liebt mich,
Ja, Jesus liebt mich,
Ja, Jesus liebt mich,
Die Bibel sagt mir dies.

JESUS LOVES ME
7.7.7.7 with Refrain

CD # 3 Tracks 9-12

Jesus Shall Reign Where'er the Sun

Isaac Watts, 1719
Based on Psalm 72

John Hamilton, 1793

D A G D A A7
1.Je - sus shall reign wher - e'er the sun
2.To Him shall end - less prayer be made,
3.Peo - ple and realms of ev - ery tongue
4.Bless - ings a - bound wher - e'er He reigns;
5.Let ev - ery crea - ture rise and bring
D G D Em Bm A
Does his suc - ces - sive jour - neys run;
And prais - es throng to crown His head;
Dwell on His love with sweet - est song,
The pris - oner leaps to lose his chains,
Pe - cul - iar hon - ors to our King,
D A D G Bm A
His king - dom stretch from shore to shore,
His Name, like sweet per - fume, shall rise
And in - fant voic - es shall pro - claim
The wea - ry find e - ter - nal rest,
An - gels de - scend with songs a - gain
D G D G D A D
till moons shall wax and wane no more.
With ev - ery morn - ing sac - ri - fice.
Their ear - ly bless - ings on His Name.
And all the sons of want are blest.
And earth re - peat the loud A - men.

DUKE STREET
L.M.

CD # 3 Tracks 13-16

Joy to the World!

Isaac Watts, 1719

Lowell Mason, 1830

D A D G D A7 D G
1.Joy to the world! the Lord is come. Let earth re -
2.Joy to the earth! the Sav - ior reigns. Let men their
3.He rules the world with truth and grace, And makes the
A7 D
ceive her King; Let ev - ery heart pre - pare Him room,
songs em - ploy, While fields and floods, rocks, hills, and plains
na - tions prove The glo - ries of His right - eous - ness
A
And heav'n and na - ture sing, And heav'n and na - ture
Re - peat the sound - ing joy, Re - peat the sound - ing
And won - ders of His love, And won - ders of His
1.And heaven and na - ture sing, And
A7 D G D G D A7 D
sing, And hea - ven and heav - en and na - ture sing.
joy, Re - peat, re - peat the sound - ing joy.
love And won - ders, won - ders of His love.
heaven and na - ture sing,

ANTIOCH
C.M.,6 lines

CD # 3 Tracks 17-20

Joyful, Joyful, We Adore Thee

Henry Van Dyke, 1852-1933 | Ludwig Van Beethoven, 1770-1827

G D7 G D G D G D
1. Joy - ful, joy - ful, we a - dore Thee, God of glo - ry, Lord of love;
2. All Thy works with joy sur - round Thee, Earth and heav'n re - flect Thy rays,
3. Thou art giv - ing and for - giv - ing, Ev - er bless - ing, ev - er blest,
4. Mor - tals join the might - y cho - rus, Which the morn - ing stars be - gan;
G G7 C G D G D G
Hearts un - fold like flow'rs be - fore Thee, Open - ing to the sun a - bove.
Stars and an - gels sing a - round Thee, Cen - ter of un - bro - ken praise;
Well - spring of the joy of liv - ing, O - cean depth of hap - py rest!
Fa - ther love is reign - ing o'er us, Broth - er love binds man to man.
D G D G D G B7 Em Am D
Melt the clouds of sin and sad - ness; Drive the dark of doubt a - way;
Field and for - est, vale and moun - tain, Flow - ery mead - ow, flash - ing sea,
Thou our Fa - ther, Christ our Broth - er All who live in love are Thine;
Ev - er sing - ing, march we on - ward, Vic - tors in the midst of strife;
G C G D7 G C G
Giv - er of im - mor - tal glad - ness, Fill us with the light of day!
Chant - ing bird and flow - ing foun - tain, Call us to re - joice in Thee.
Teach us how to love each oth - er, Lift us to the Joy Di - vine.
Joy - ful mu - sic leads us sun - ward In the tri - umph song of life. A - men.

HYMN TO JOY
8.7.8.7.

CD # 3 Tracks 21-24

Just As I Am

Charlotte Elliott, 1789-1871

William B. Bradbury, 1816-1868

E♭ B♭ E♭
1. Just as I am, with - out one plea,
2. Just as I am, and wait - ing not
3. Just as I am, though tossed a - bout
4. Just as I am, poor, wretch - ed, blind;
5. Just as I am, Thou wilt re - ceive,
B♭ B♭ A♭ E♭
But that Thy blood was shed for me, And that Thou bidd'st me
To rid my soul of one dark blot, To Thee whose blood can
With many a con - flict, many a doubt, Fight - ings and fears with -
Sight, rich - es, heal - ing of the mind Yea, all I need, in
Wilt wel - come, par - don, cleanse, re - lieve; Be - cause Thy prom - ise
A♭ E♭ A♭ B♭ E♭ A♭ E♭
come to Thee, O Lamb of God, I come, I come!
cleanse each spot, O Lamb of God, I come, I come!
in, with - out, O Lamb of God, I come, I come!
Thee to find, O Lamb of God, I come, I come! A - men.
I be - lieve, O Lamb of God, I come, I come!

WOODWORTH
L.M.

CD # 3 Tracks 25-28

Lead On, O King Eternal

Ernest W. Shurtleff, 1888 — Henry Smart, 1836

D G D G D A D G
1. Lead on, O King E - ter - nal, The day of march has come; Hence-forth in fields of
2. Lead on, O King, E - ter - nal, Till sin's fierce war shall cease, And ho - li - ness shall
3. Lead on, O King, E - ter - nal, We fol - low, not with fears; For glad-ness breaks like
D A E7 A D G
con - quest Thy tents shall be our home. Thro' days of prep - a - ra - tion Thy
whis - per The sweet A - men of peace; For not with swords loud clash - ing, Nor
morn - ing Wher - e'er Thy face ap - pears; Thy cross is lift - ed o'er us; We
E A D G D A7 D G D
grace has made us strong, And now, O King E - ter - nal, We lift our bat - tle song.
roll of stir-ring drums; With deeds of love and mer - cy, The heav'n-ly king dom comes.
jour-ney in its light: The crown a-waits the con-quest; Lead on, O God of might. A-MEN.

LANCASHIRE
7. 6. 7. 6. D.

CD # 3 Tracks 29-32

Lift High the Cross

George William Ketchin and
Michael Robert Newbolt, 1916, alt.

Sydney Hugo Nicholson, 1916

C Dm C G
Refrain (Unison)
Lift high the cross, the love of Christ pro - claim
C F G Dm G7 C
Fine
till all the world a - dore his sa - cred name.
Em Am D G C Am B Em
Harmony
1. Come, Chris - tians, fol - low this tri - um - phant sign. The
2. Each new - born ser - vant of the Cru - ci - fied bears
3. O Lord, once lift - ed on the glo - rious tree, as
4. So shall our song of tri - umph ev - er be: Praise
Am Bm G C D G
D.C.
hosts of God in u - ni - ty com - bine.
on the brow the seal of him who died.
thou hast prom - ised, draw the world to thee.
to the Cru - ci - fied for vic - to - ry!

CRUCIFER
10. 10. with Refrain

CD # 3 Tracks 33-36

Like a River Glorious

Frances R. Havergal, 1836-1879

James Mountain, 1843-1933

1. Like a river glorious Is God's perfect peace, O - ver all victorious In its bright increase; Perfect, yet it floweth Fuller ev'ry day; Perfect, yet it groweth Deeper all the way.
2. Hidden in the hollow Of His blessed hand, Never foe can follow, Never traitor stand; Not a surge of worry, Not a shade of care, Not a blast of hurry Touch the spirit there.
3. Ev'ry joy or trial Falleth from above, Trac'd upon our dial By the sun of Love; We may trust Him fully All for us to do; They who trust Him wholly Find Him wholly true.
Stayed upon Jehovah, Hearts are fully blest;
Finding, as He promised, Perfect peace and rest.

WYE VALLEY
6. 5. 6. 5. D. with Refrain

CD # 3 Tracks 37-40

Lord Jesus, I Long to Be Perfectly Whole

James Nicholson
William G. Fischer

1. Lord Je-sus, I long to be per-fect-ly whole; I want Thee for-ev-er to live in my soul; Break down ev-'ry i-dol, cast out ev-'ry foe; Now wash me, and I shall be whit-er than snow.
2. Lord Je-sus, look down from Thy throne in the skies, And help me to make a com-plete sac-ri-fice; I give up my-self, and what-ev-er I know,
3. Lord Je-sus, for this I most hum-bly en-treat, I wait, bless-ed Lord, at Thy cru-ci-fied feet; By faith, for my cleans-ing, I see Thy blood flow,
4. Lord Je-sus, Thou see-est I pa-tient-ly wait, Come now, and with-in me a new heart cre-ate; To those who have sought Thee, Thou ne-ver saidst "No,"
Refrain
Whit-er than snow, yes, whit-er than snow; Now wash me, and I shall be whit-er than snow.

CD # 3 Tracks 45-48

FISCHER
11.11.11.11. with Refrain

Low in the Grave He Lay

Robert Lowry, 1874 | Robert Lowry, 1874

1.Low in the grave He lay - Je - sus, my Sav - ior; Wait - ing the coming day - Je - sus, my Lord.
2.Vain - ly they watch His bed - Je - sus, my Sav - ior; Vain - ly they seal the dead - Je - sus, my Lord.
3.Death can - not keep his prey - Je - sus, my Sav - ior; He tore the bars a - way - Je - sus my Lord.
Up from the grave He a - rose, With a might - y tri - umph o'er His foes.
He a-rose!
He a - rose a Vic - tor from the dark do - main,
He a-rose!
And He lives for - ev - er with His saints to reign.
He a - rose! He a - rose! Hal - le - lu - jah! Christ a - rose!
He a-rose! He a-rose!

CHRIST AROSE
6.5.6.4. with Refrain

CD # 3 Tracks 41-44

"Man of Sorrows," What a Name

Philip P. Bliss | Philip P. Bliss, 1875

C Am E F C G D7 G
1. Man of Sor - rows! what a name for the Son of God, who came
2. Bear - ing shame and scoff - ing rude, in my place con - demned He stood;
3. Guilt - y, vile, and help - less we; spot - less Lamb of God was He;
4. Lift - ed up was He to die; "It is fin - ished!" was His cry;
5. When He comes, our glo - rious King, all His ran - somed home to bring,
C F C C G C G7 Am F C
ru - ined sin - ners to re - claim, Hal - le - lu - jah! What a Sav - ior.
sealed my par - don with His blood, Hal - le - lu - jah! What a Sav - ior!
full a - tone - ment can it be? Hal - le - lu - jah! What a Sav - ior!
now in heaven ex - alt - ed high, Hal - le - lu - jah! What a Sav - ior!
then a - new this song we'll sing: Hal - le - lu - jah! What a Sav - ior!

HALLELUJAH! WHAT A SAVIOR
7.7.7.8

CD # 3 Tracks 49-52

My Faith Has Found a Resting Place

Lidie H. Edmonds

Arr. by William J. Kirkpatrick

G C Am G D7 G
1. My faith has found a rest-ing place, Not in de-vice nor deed;
2. E - nough for me that Je-sus saves, this ends my fear and doubt;
3. My heart is lean - ing on the Word, The writ-ten Word of God,
4. My great Phy - si - cian heals the sick, The lost He came to save;
C Am G D7 G
I trust the Ev - er - liv - ing One, His wounds for me shall plead.
A sin - ful soul I come to Him, He'll nev - er cast me out.
Sal - va - tion by my Sav - iour's name, Sal - va - tion thro' His blood.
for me His pre - cious blood He shed, For me His life He gave.
CHORUS
D7 G C G D7
I need no oth - er ar - gu-ment, I need no oth - er plea,
G C Am G D7 G
It is e-nough that Je - sus died, And that He died for me.

LANDAS
C.M. with Refrain

CD # 3 Tracks 53-56

My Jesus, I Love Thee

William R. Featherstone, 1842-1878

Adoniram J. Gordon, 1836-1895

1. My Je - sus, I love Thee, I know Thou art mine,
2. I love Thee be - cause Thou hast first lov - ed me,
3. I'll love Thee in life, I will love Thee in death,
4. In man - sions of glo - ry and end - less de - light
For Thee all the fol - lies of sin I re - sign;
And pur - chased my par - don on Cal - va - ry's tree;
And praise Thee as long as Thou lend - est me breath;
I'll ev - er a - dore Thee in heav - en so bright;
My gra - cious Re - deem - er my Sav - iour art Thou;
I love Thee for wear - ing the thorns on Thy brow;
And say when the death dew lies cold on my brow,
I'll sing with the glit - ter - ing crown on my brow,
If ev - er I loved Thee, my Je - sus, 'tis now.
If ev - er I loved Thee, my Je - sus, 'tis now.
If ev - er I loved Thee, my Je - sus, 'tis now.
If ev - er I loved Thee, my Je - sus, 'tis now. A - MEN.

GORDON
11. 11. 11. 11.

CD # 3 Tracks 57-60

Nearer, Still Nearer

Mrs. C.H. Morris, 1862-1929 | Mrs. C.H. Morris, 1862-1929

1. Near - er, still near - er, close to Thy heart, Draw me, my
2. Near - er, still near - er, noth - ing I bring, Naught as an
3. Near - er, still near - er, Lord, to be Thine, Sin with its
4. Near - er, still near - er, while life shall last, Till safe in
Sav - ior, so pre - cious Thou art; Fold me, O fold me
of - f'ring to Je - sus my King; On - ly my sin - ful,
fol - lies I glad - ly re - sign; All of its pleas - ures,
glo - ry my an - chor is cast; Thro' end - less a - ges,
close to Thy breast, Shel - ter me safe in that ha - ven of rest,
now con - trite heart; Grant me the cleans - ing Thy blood doth im - part,
pomp, and its pride; Give me but Je - sus, my Lord cru - ci - fied,
ev - er to be, Near - er, my Sav - ior, still near - er to Thee,
Shel - ter me safe in that ha - ven of rest.
Grant me the cleans - ing Thy blood doth im - part.
Give me but Je - sus, my Lord cru - ci - fied.
Near - er, my Sav - iour, still near - er to Thee. A - MEN.

MORRIS.
9. 10. 9. 10.

CD # 4 Tracks 1-4

O Come, All Ye Faithful

Anonymous. Latin, Eighteenth Century
Tr. by Frederick Oakeley, 1802-1880, and others

From John F. Wade's Cantus Diversi, 1751

G D D7 G D G C G D Em7 A7 D A7
1. O come, all ye faith - ful, joy - ful and tri - um - phant, O come ye, O
2. Sing, choirs of an - gels, sing in ex - ul - ta - tion, O sing, all ye
3. Yea, Lord, we greet Thee, born this hap - py morn - ing, Je - sus, to
D G D G D A7 D G D7 G D7 G D G Em Am
come ye to Beth - le - hem! Come and be - hold Him, born the King of
bright hosts of heav'n a - bove! Glo - ry to God, all glo - ry in the
Thee be all glor - ry giv'n; Word of the Fa - ther, now in flesh ap -
D G D G D7 G D G D7 G D
Refrain
an - gels!
high - est! O come, let us a - dore Him, O come, let us a - dore Him,
pear - ing!
G D7 G D A7 D G C G D7 G C G
O come, let us a - dore Him, Christ the Lord! A - MEN.

ADESTE FIDELES.
IRREGULAR WITH REFRAIN

CD # 4 Tracks 5-8

O for a Thousand Tongues to Sing

Charles Wesley, 1707-1788

Carl G. Glaser, 1784-1829
Arr. by Lowell Mason, 1792-1872

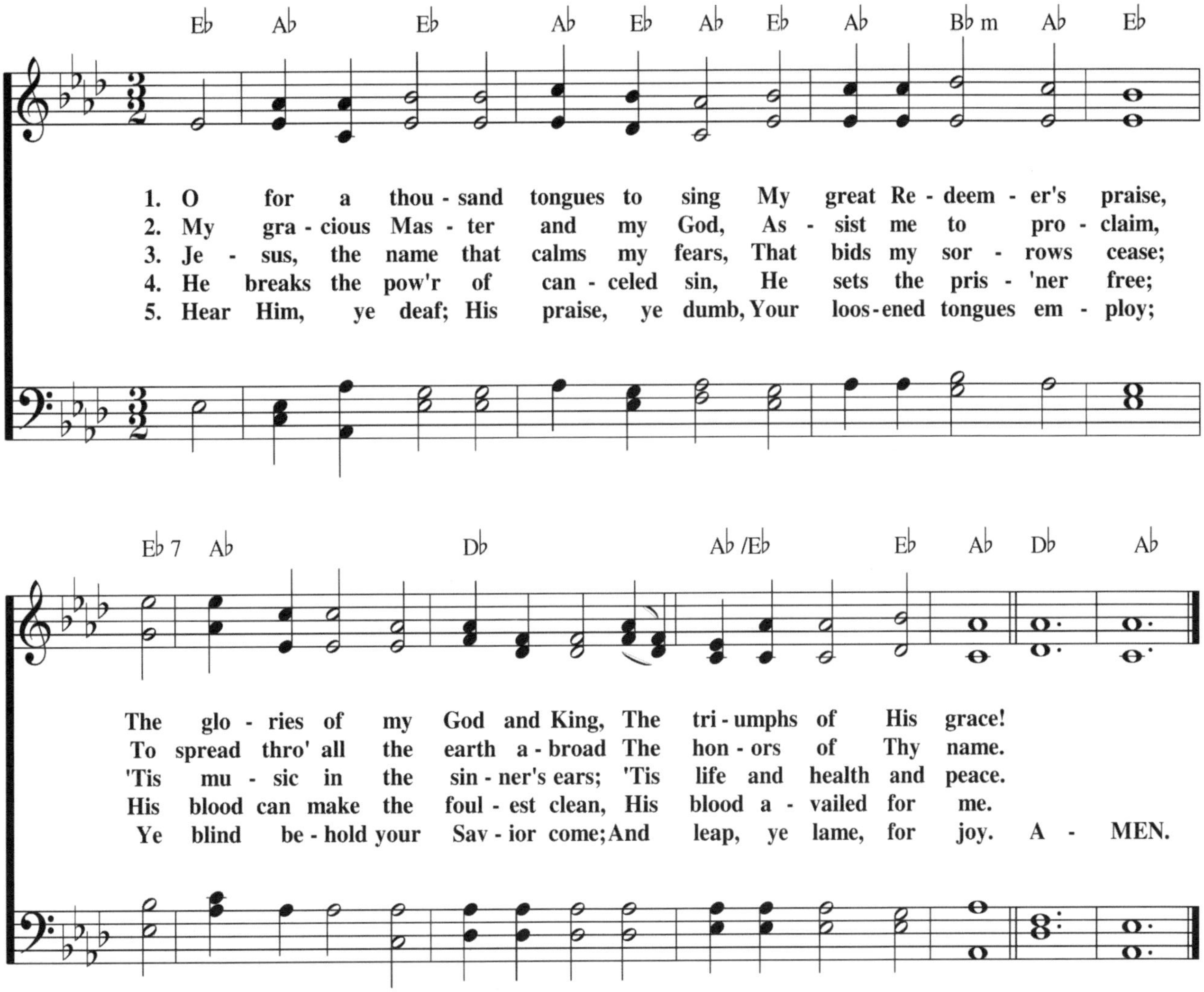
Eb Ab Eb Ab Eb Ab Eb Ab Bb m Ab Eb
1. O for a thou - sand tongues to sing My great Re - deem - er's praise,
2. My gra - cious Mas - ter and my God, As - sist me to pro - claim,
3. Je - sus, the name that calms my fears, That bids my sor - rows cease;
4. He breaks the pow'r of can - celed sin, He sets the pris - 'ner free;
5. Hear Him, ye deaf; His praise, ye dumb, Your loos-ened tongues em - ploy;
Eb 7 Ab Db Ab /Eb Eb Ab Db Ab
The glo - ries of my God and King, The tri - umphs of His grace!
To spread thro' all the earth a - broad The hon - ors of Thy name.
'Tis mu - sic in the sin - ner's ears; 'Tis life and health and peace.
His blood can make the foul - est clean, His blood a - vailed for me.
Ye blind be - hold your Sav - ior come; And leap, ye lame, for joy. A - MEN.

AZMON
C.M.

CD # 4 Tracks 9-12

O Worship the King, All Glorious Above

Robert Grant, 1833

J. Michael Haydn, 1770

G D G C D G D
1.O wor - ship the King, all - glo - rious a - bove,
2.O tell of His might, O sing of His grace,
3.Thy boun - ti - ful care what tongue can re - cite?
4.Frail chil - dren of dust, and fee - ble as frail,
G D G C G D G
O grate - ful - ly sing His power and His love;
Whose robe is the light, whose can - o - py space.
It breathes in the air, it shines in the light;
In Thee do we trust, nor find Thee to fail;
D G D G D7
Our Shield and De - fend - er, the An - cient of Days,
His char - iots of wrath the deep thun - der - clouds form,
It streams from the hills, it de - scends to the plain,
Thy mer - cies how ten - der, how firm to the end!
G D G Am7 G D7 G
Pa - vil - ioned in splend - dor, and gird - ed with praise.
And dark is His path on the wings of the storm.
And sweet - ly dis - tills in the dew and the rain.
Our Mak - er, De - fend - er, Re - deem - er and Friend.

LYONS
10.10.11.11.

CD # 4 Tracks 13-16

Onward, Christian Soldiers

Sabine Baring-Gould

Arthur S. Sullivan

Eb Fm Bb7 Bb Eb Eb/G Fsus7 Bb
1. On - ward, Christ-ian sol - diers, March-ing as to war, With the cross of Je - sus
2. Like a might - y ar - my Moves the church of God; Broth-ers, we are tread - ing
3. Crowns and thrones may per - ish king-doms rise and wane; But the Church of Je - sus
4. On - ward, then, ye peo - ple, join our hap - py throng, Blend with ours your voi - ces
F7 Bb Eb Ab
go - ing on be - fore! Christ, the roy - al Mas - ter, Leads a-gainst the foe;
where the saints have trod; We are not di - vid - ed; All one bod - y we,
con - stant will re - main; Gates of hell can nev – er 'gainst that Church pre - vail;
in the tri - umph song; Glo - ry, laud, and hon – or un - to Christ the King;
Eb Ab Eb Ab Eb Fm F9 Bb Eb Fm Bb7
Refrain
For-ward in - to bat - tle, See His ban-ner go!
One in hope and doc - trine, One in char - i - ty.
We have Christ's own prom - ise, and that can-not fail.
This thro' count - less a - ges men and an-gels sing.
On-ward, Christ - ian sold - diers,
Bb7 Eb Fm Bb7 Eb/G Ab Bb7 Eb
March-ing as to war, With the cross of Je - sus Go-ing on be - fore!

ST. GERTRUDE
6. 5. 6. 5. D. with Refrain

CD # 4 Tracks 17-20

Praise to the Lord, the Almighty

Joachim Neander, 1680
Trans. by Catherine Winkworth, 1863

Stralsund Gesangbuch, 1665

G Em D/F♯ G D Em G/B C G C Am Em Em C6 D
1.Praise to the Lord, the Al - might - y, the King of cre - a -
2.Praise to the Lord, who o'er all things so won - drous - ly reign -
3.Praise to the Lord, who doth pros - per thy work and de - fend
4.Praise to the Lord! O let all that is in me a - dore
G Em D/F♯ G D Em G/B C G C Am Em
tion! O my soul, praise Him, for He is thy health and sal -
eth, Shel - ters thee un - der His wings, yea, so gen - tly sus -
thee; Sure - ly His good - ness and mer - cy here dai - ly at -
Him! All that hath life and breath, come now with prais - es be -
C6 D G G D/F♯ G C G Em D/F♯ G Am G
va - tion! All ye who hear, Now to His tem - ple draw
tain - eth! Hast thou not seen How thy de - sires e'er have
tend thee. Pon - der a - new What the Al - might - y can
fore Him! Let the A - men Sound from His peo - ple a -
D G/B C Am Em C D C6 D G
near; Join me in glad ad - o - ra - tion!
been Grant - ed in what He or - dain - eth?
do, If with His love He be - friend thee.
gain: Glad - ly for aye we a - dore Him. A - men.

LOBE DEN HERREN
14.14.4.7.8.

CD # 4 Tracks 21-24

Rock of Ages, Cleft for Me

Augustus M. Toplady, 1740-1778, Alt.   Thomas Hastings, 1784-1872

B♭ E♭ B♭ F7 B♭
1. Rock of A - ges, cleft for me, Let me hide my - self in Thee;
2. Not the la - bors of my hands Can ful - fill Thy law's de - mands;
3. Noth - ing in my hand I bring, Sim - ply to Thy cross I cling;
4. While I draw this fleet - ing breath, When my eye - lids close in death,
F B♭ F B♭
Let the wa - ter and the blood, From Thy wound - ed side which flowed,
Could my zeal no lan - guor know, Could my tears for - ever - er flow,
Na - ked, come to Thee for dress; Help - less, look to Thee for grace;
When I soar to worlds un - known, See Thee on Thy judg - ment throne,
E♭ B♭ E♭ 7 B♭ F7 B♭
Be of sin the dou - ble cure, Save from guilt and make me pure.
All for sin could not - a - tone; Thou must save and Thou a - lone.
Foul, I to the foun - tain fly; Wash me, Sav - ior, or I die.
Rock of A - ges, cleft for me, Let me hide me - self in Thee.

TOPLADY
7. 7. 7. 7. 7. 7.

CD # 4 Tracks 25-28

Silent Night, Holy Night

Joseph Mohr, 1792-1848

Franz Gruber, 1787-1863

B♭ F7 F B♭
1. Si - lent night, ho - ly night, All is calm, all is bright
2. Si - lent night, ho - ly night, Shep - herds quake at the sight!
3. Si - lent night, ho - ly night, Son of God, love's pure light
4. Si - lent night, ho - ly night, Won - drous Star, lend thy light;
E♭ B♭ E♭ B♭ E♭
Round yon Vir - gin Moth - er and child! Ho - ly In - fant so
Glo - ries stream from heaven a - far, Heaven - ly hosts sing
Ra - diant beams from Thy ho - ly face, With the dawn of re -
With the an - gels let us sing, Al - le - lu - ia
B♭ E♭ B♭ F7
ten - der and mild, Sleep in heav - en - ly
"Al - le - lu - ia! Christ the Sav - ior is
deem - ing grace, Je - sus. Lord, at Thy
to our King; Christ the Sav - ior is
B♭ Dm F7 B♭
peace, Sleep in heav - en - ly peace.
born, Christ the Sav - ior is born."
birth, Je - sus, Lord, at Thy birth.
born, Christ the Sav - ior is born.

STILLE NACHT
Irregular

CD # 4 Tracks 29-32

Stand Up, Stand Up for Jesus

George Duffield, Jr., 1818-1888 | George J. Webb, 1803-1887

1. Stand up, stand up for Je - sus, Ye sol - diers of the cross;
2. Stand up, stand up for Je - sus, Stand in His strength a - lone;
3. Stand up, stand up for Je - sus, The strife will not be long;
Lift high His roy - al ban - ner, It must not suf - fer loss:
The arm of flesh will fail you, Ye dare not trust your own:
This day the noise of bat - tle, The next the vic - tor's song:
From vic - t'ry un - to vic - t'ry His ar - my shall He lead,
Put on the gos - pel ar - mor, Each piece put on with prayer,
To him that o - ver - com - eth A crown of life shall be;
Till ev - 'ry foe is van - quished, And Christ is Lord in - deed.
Where du - ty calls or dan - ger, Be nev - er want - ing there.
He, with the King of glo - ry, Shall reign e - ter - nal - ly.

WEBB
7.6.7.6.D.

CD # 4 Tracks 33-36

Take My Life, and Let It Be

Frances R. Havergal, 1836-1879 | Henri A. Cesar Malan, 1787-1860

F C F Dm Gm
1. Take my life and let it be Con - se - crat- ed,
2. Take my hands and let them move At the im- pulse
3. Take my voice and let me sing Al - ways, on - ly,
4. Take my sil - ver and my gold; Not a mite would
5. Take my will and make it Thine; It shall be no
6. Take my love; my Lord, I pour At Thy feet its
F C F C B♭ F B♭
Lord, to Thee; Take my mo - ments and my days; Let them flow in
of thy love. Take my feet, and let them be Swift and beau - ti -
for my King. Take my lips, and let them be Filled with mes - sag -
I with- hold. Take my in - tell - ect, and use Ev - 'ry power as
lon - ger mine. Take my heart, it is Thine own; It shall be Thy
trea - sure store. Take my - self, and I will be Ev - er, on - ly,
Gm C F Dm F C F
end - less praise, Let them flow in end - less praise.
ful for Thee, Swift and beau - ti - ful for Thee.
es from Thee, Filled with mes - sa - ges from Thee.
Thou shalt choose, Ev - 'ry power as Thou shalt choose.
roy - al throne, It shall be Thy roy - al throne.
all for Thee, Ev - er, on - ly, all for Thee.

HENDON.
7.7.7.7.7.7.

CD # 4 Tracks 37-40

The Church's One Foundation

Samuel J. Stone, 1839-1900

Samuel S. Wesley, 1810-1876

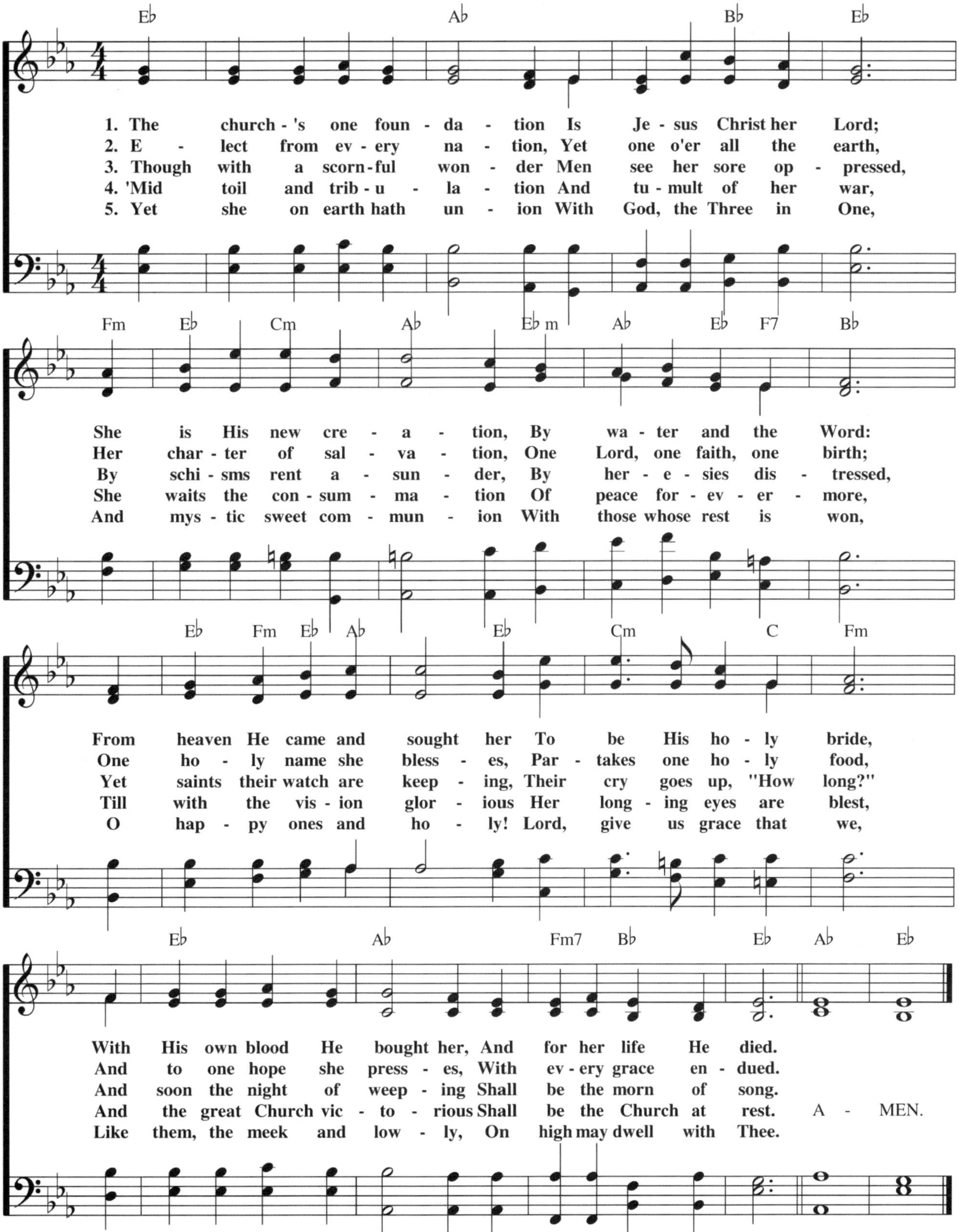
Eb Ab Bb Eb
1. The church - 's one foun - da - tion Is Je - sus Christ her Lord;
2. E - lect from ev - ery na - tion, Yet one o'er all the earth,
3. Though with a scorn - ful won - der Men see her sore op - pressed,
4. 'Mid toil and trib - u - la - tion And tu - mult of her war,
5. Yet she on earth hath un - ion With God, the Three in One,
Fm Eb Cm Ab Eb m Ab Eb F7 Bb
She is His new cre - a - tion, By wa - ter and the Word:
Her char - ter of sal - va - tion, One Lord, one faith, one birth;
By schi - sms rent a - sun - der, By her - e - sies dis - tressed,
She waits the con - sum - ma - tion Of peace for - ev - er - more,
And mys - tic sweet com - mun - ion With those whose rest is won,
Eb Fm Eb Ab Eb Cm C Fm
From heaven He came and sought her To be His ho - ly bride,
One ho - ly name she bless - es, Par - takes one ho - ly food,
Yet saints their watch are keep - ing, Their cry goes up, "How long?"
Till with the vis - ion glor - ious Her long - ing eyes are blest,
O hap - py ones and ho - ly! Lord, give us grace that we,
Eb Ab Fm7 Bb Eb Ab Eb
With His own blood He bought her, And for her life He died.
And to one hope she press - es, With ev - ery grace en - dued.
And soon the night of weep - ing Shall be the morn of song.
And the great Church vic - to - rious Shall be the Church at rest. A - MEN.
Like them, the meek and low - ly, On high may dwell with Thee.

AURELIA
7.6.7.6.D.

CD # 4 Tracks 41-44

The Ends of All the Earth Shall Hear

PSALM 22

William H. Doane, 1834-1915

E♭ A♭ E♭
1.The ends of all the earth shall hear And turn un - to the
2.For His the king - dom, His of right, He rules the na - tions
3.Both rich and poor, both bond and free Shall wor - ship Him on
4.The Lord's un - fail - ing right - eous - ness All gen - er - a - tions
B♭7 E♭ A♭ E♭
Lord in fear; All kin - dreds of the earth shall own
by His might; All earth to Him her hom - age brings,
bend - ed knee, And child - ren's child - ren shall pro - claim
shall con - fess, From age to age shall men be taught
A♭ E♭ B♭
Refrain
And wor - ship Him as God a - lone.
The Lord of lords, the King of kings. All earth to Him
The glor - ious hon - or of His Name.
What wond - rous works the Lord has wrought.
A♭ E♭ A♭ E♭ B♭7 E♭
her hom - age brings, The Lord of lords the King of kings.

VISION
10.10.9.10.

CD # 4 Tracks 45-48

The Solid Rock

Edward Mote, 1797-1874

William B. Bradbury, 1816-1868

F C F B♭ Gm C F
1. My hope is built on noth-ing less Than Je-sus' blood and right-eous-ness;
2. When dark-ness seems to hide His face, I rest on His un - chang-ing grace;
3. His oath, His cov - e - nant, His blood Sup - port me in the whelm-ing flood;
4. When He shall come with trum-pet sound, Oh, may I then in Him be found;
C F B♭ Gm C F
I dare not trust the sweet-est frame, But whol-ly lean on Je-sus' name.
In ev-ery high and storm-y gale, My an-chor hold with - in the vail.
When all a-round my soul gives way, He then is all my hope and stay.
Dressed in His right-eous - ness a - lone, Fault - less to stand be - fore the throne.
Refrain
B♭ F
On Christ, the sol - id Rock, I stand; All oth - er ground is
C F B♭ F C7 F
sink - ing sand, All oth - er ground is sink - ing sand.

SOLID ROCK.
L. M. with Refrain

CD # 4 Tracks 49-52

This Is My Father's World

Maltbie D. Babcock, 1858-1901 | Franklin L. Sheppard, 1852-1930

1. This is my Fa - ther's world, And to my lis - t'ning ears, All
2. This is my Fa - ther's world, The birds their car - ols raise; The
3. This is my Fa - ther's world, O let me ne'er for - get That
na - ture sings, and round me rings The mus - ic of the spheres.
morn - ing light, the lil - y white De - clare their Ma - ker's praise.
though the wrong seems oft so strong, God is the Rul - er yet.
This is my Fa - ther's world, I rest me in the thought Of
This is my Fa - ther's world, He shines in all that's fair; In the
This is my Fa - ther's world, Why should my heart be sad? The
rocks and trees, of skies and seas His hand the won - ders wrought.
rust - ling grass I hear Him pass, He speaks to me ev - 'ry - where.
Lord is King, let the heav - ens ring! God reigns; let the earth be glad.

TERRA PATRIS.
S. M. D.

CD # 4 Tracks 53-56

We Gather Together

Netherlands folk hymn
Trans. by Theodore Baker, 1917

Nederlandtsch Gedenckelanck, 1626
Arr. by Edward Kremser, 1877

D A7 D Em A D
1.We gath - er to - geth - er to ask the Lord's bless - ing;
2.Be - side us to guide us, our God with us join - ing,
3.We all do ex - tol Thee, Thou Lead - er tri - um - phant,
A D E A7 A
He chast - ens and hast - ens His will to make known;
Or - dain - ing, main - tain - ing His king - dom di - vine;
And pray that Thou still our De - fend - er wilt be.
A7 D Em A D
The wick - ed op - ress - ing now cease from dis - tress - ing;
So from the be - gin - ning the fight we were win - ning; -
Let Thy con - gre - ga - tion es - cape trib - u - la - tion;
G A D Em A D
Sing prais - es to His Name; He for - gets not His own.
Thou, Lord, wast at our side; all glo - ry be Thine!
Thy Name be ev - er praised! O Lord, make us free!

KREMSER
12.11.12.11.

CD # 4 Tracks 57-60

We Have Heard the Joyful Sound

Priscilla J. Owens, 1829-1907 | William J. Kirkpatrick, 1838-1921

G
D7
1. We have heard the joy - ful sound: Je - sus saves! Je - sus saves!
2. Waft it on the roll - ing tide: Je - sus saves! Je - sus saves!
3. Sing a - bove the bat - tle strife: Je - sus saves! Je - sus saves!
4. Give the winds a might - y voice: Je - sus saves! Je - sus saves!
G
D7
G
Spread the ti - dings all a - round: Je - sus saves! Je - sus saves!
Tell to sin - ners far and wide: Je - sus saves! Je - sus saves!
By His death and end - less life, Je - sus saves! Je - sus saves!
Let the na - tions now re - joice, Je - sus saves! Je - sus saves!
C
G
D
Bear the news to ev - ery land, climb the steeps and cross the waves;
Sing, ye is - lands of the sea; Ech - o back, ye o - cean caves;
Sing it soft - ly through the gloom, when the heart for mer - cy craves;
Shout sal - va - tion full and free; High - est hills and deep - est caves;
G
C
G
D7
G
On - ward! 'tis our Lord's com - mand; Je - sus saves! Je - sus saves!
Earth shall keep her ju - bi - lee: Je - sus saves! Je - sus saves!
Sing in tri - umph o'er the tomb, Je - sus saves! Je - sus saves!
This our song of vic - to - ry: Je - sus saves! Je - sus saves!

JESUS SAVES
7. 6. 7. 6. 7. 7. 7. 6.

CD # 4 Tracks 61-64

What a Fellowship, What a Joy Divine

Elisha A. Hoffman, 1839-1929

Anthony J. Showalter, 1858-1924

G C G D
1. What a fel - low - ship, what a joy di - vine, Lean - ing on the ev - er - last-ing arms;
2. Oh, how sweet to walk in this pil - grim way, Lean - ing on the ev - er - last-ing arms;
3. What have I to dread, what have I to fear, Lean - ing on the ev - er - last-ing arms?
G C G D7 G
What a bless - ed - ness, what a peace is mine, Lean - ing on the ev - er - last - ing arms.
Oh, how bright the path grows from day to day, Lean - ing on the ev - er - last - ing arms.
I have bless - ed peace with my Lord so near, Lean - ing on the ev - er - last - ing arms.
C G D
Lean - ing, lean - ing, Safe and se - cure from all a - larms;
Lean - ing on Je - sus, lean - ing on Je - sus,
G C G D7 G
Lean - ing, lean - ing, Lean - ing on the ev - er - last - ing arms.
Lean - ing on Je - sus, lean - ing on Je - sus,

SHOWALTER
10. 9. 10. 9. with Refrain

CD # 5 Tracks 1-4

What a Friend We Have in Jesus

Joseph Scriven, 1820-1886

Charles C. Converse, 1832-1918

F Bb F C7
1. What a friend we have in Je - sus, All our sins and griefs to bear!
2. Have we tri - als and temp - ta - tions? Is there trou-ble an - y - where?
3. Are we weak and heav - y lad - en, Cum-bered with a load of care?
F Bb F C7 F
What a priv - i - lege to car - ry Ev - 'ry-thing to God in prayer!
We should nev - er be dis - cour - aged, Take it to the Lord in prayer:
Pre - cious Sav-iour, still our ref - uge; Take it to the Lord in prayer:
C F Bb F C7
Oh, what peace we of - ten for - feit, Oh, what need-less pain we bear,
Can we find a friend so faith - ful Who will all our sor-rows share?
Do thy friends de - spise, for - sake thee? Take it to the Lord in prayer;
F Bb F C7 F
All be - cause we do not car - ry Ev - 'ry-thing to God in prayer!
Je - sus knows our ev - 'ry weak - ness, Take it to the Lord in prayer.
in His arms He'll take and shield thee; Thou wilt find a sol - ace there.

CONVERSE
8. 7. 8. 7. D.

CD # 5 Tracks 5-8

When I Survey the Wondrous Cross

Isaac Watts, 1674-1748

From a Gregorian Chant
Arr. by Lowell Mason, 1792-1872

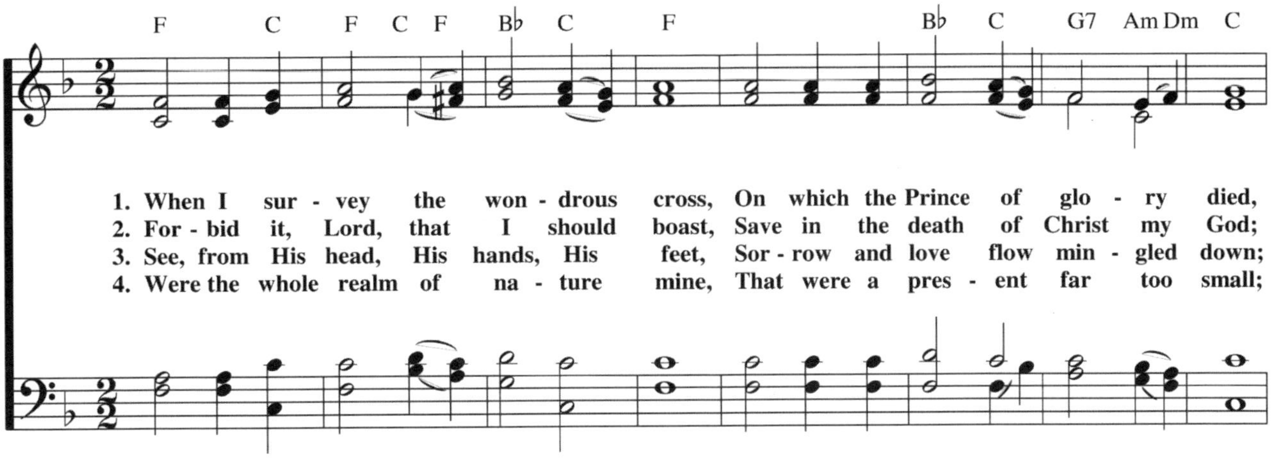
F C F C F B♭ C F B♭ C G7 Am Dm C
1. When I sur - vey the won - drous cross, On which the Prince of glo - ry died,
2. For - bid it, Lord, that I should boast, Save in the death of Christ my God;
3. See, from His head, His hands, His feet, Sor - row and love flow min - gled down;
4. Were the whole realm of na - ture mine, That were a pres - ent far too small;

F C F C F Gm C F C Dm Gm7 C F B♭ F
My rich - est gain I count but loss, And pour con - tempt on all my pride.
All the vain things that charm me most, I sac - ri - fice them to His blood.
Did e'er such love and sor - row meet, Or thorns com - pose so rich a crown.
Love so a - maz - ing, so di - vine, De - mands my soul, my life, my all. A - MEN.

HAMBURG
L. M.

CD # 5 Tracks 13-16

When Morning Gilds the Skies

From the German, c. 1800
Tr. by Edward Caswall, 1814-1878

Joseph Barnaby, 1838-1896

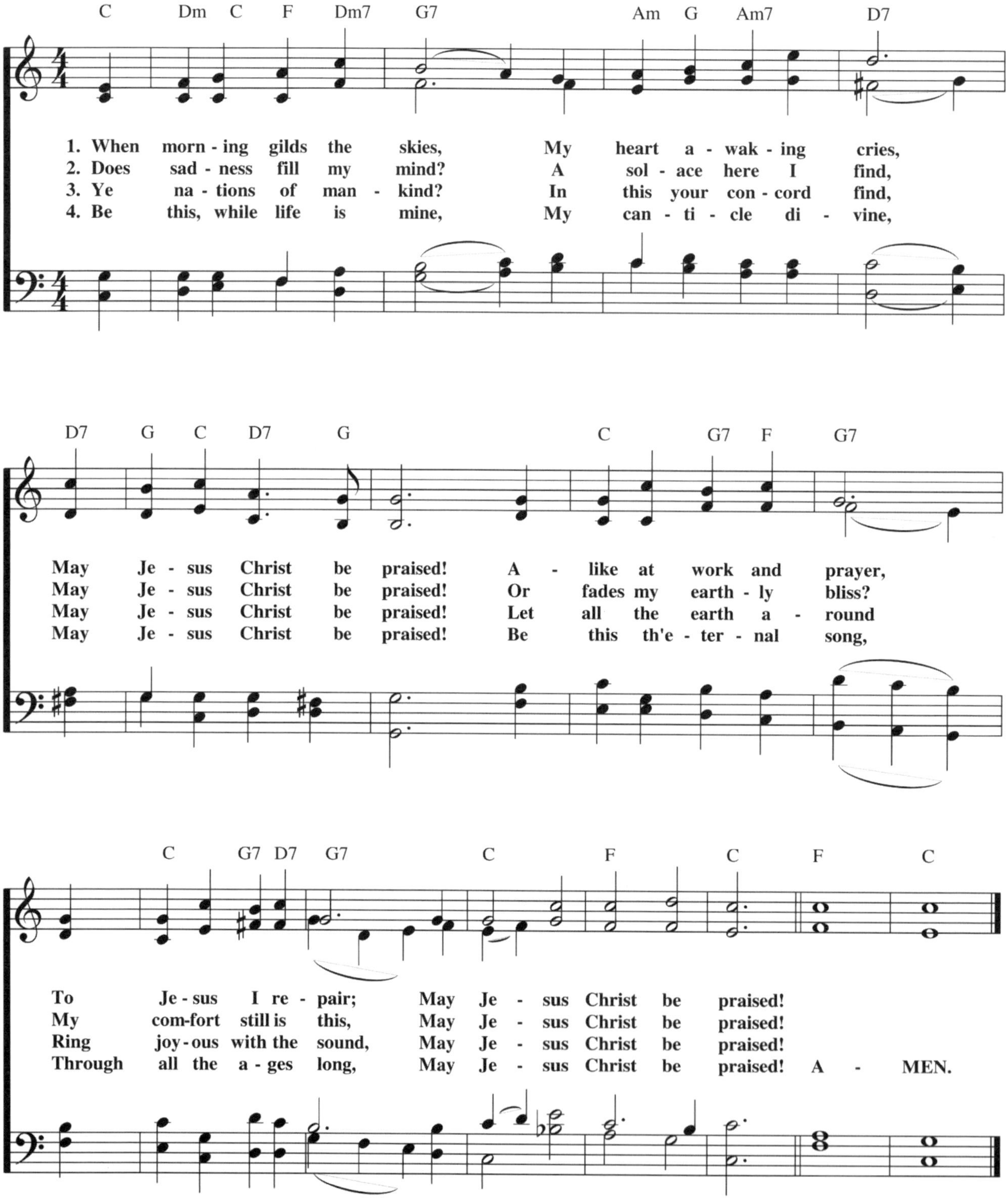
C Dm C F Dm7 G7 Am G Am7 D7
1. When morn - ing gilds the skies, My heart a - wak - ing cries,
2. Does sad - ness fill my mind? A sol - ace here I find,
3. Ye na - tions of man - kind? In this your con - cord find,
4. Be this, while life is mine, My can - ti - cle di - vine,
D7 G C D7 G C G7 F G7
May Je - sus Christ be praised! A - like at work and prayer,
May Je - sus Christ be praised! Or fades my earth - ly bliss?
May Je - sus Christ be praised! Let all the earth a - round
May Je - sus Christ be praised! Be this th'e - ter - nal song,
C G7 D7 G7 C F C F C
To Je - sus I re - pair; May Je - sus Christ be praised!
My com-fort still is this, May Je - sus Christ be praised!
Ring joy - ous with the sound, May Je - sus Christ be praised!
Through all the a - ges long, May Je - sus Christ be praised! A - MEN.

LAUDES DOMINI
6. 6. 6. 6. 6. 6.

CD # 5 Tracks 9-12

When Peace, Like a River

Horatio G. Spafford, 1828-1888

Philip P. Bliss, 1838-1876

C Dm C Dm C
1. When peace like a riv - er at - tend - eth my way, When
2. Though Sa - tan should buf - fet, though tri - als should come, Let
3. My sin oh, the bliss of this glo - ri - ous thought! My
4. O Lord, haste the day when my faith shall be sight, The
Am G Am C D G C F
sor - rows like sea bil - lows roll, What - ev - er my lot, Thou hast
this blest as - sur - ance con - trol, That Christ has re - gard - ed my
sin, not in part but the whole, Is nailed to the cross and I
clouds be rolled back as a scroll, The trump shall re - sound, and the
D G F G C F C G C
taught me to say, "It is well, it is well with my soul."
help - less es - tate, And has shed His own blood for my soul.
bear it no more! Praise the Lord, praise the Lord, O my soul!
Lord shall de - scend! E - ven so it is well with my soul!
C G G7 C F C G C
It is well with my soul; it is well, it is well with my soul!
It is well with my soul;

VILLE DU HAVRE
11. 8. 11. 9. with Refrain

CD # 5 Tracks 17-20

Whole-hearted Thanksgiving to Thee I Will Bring

PSALM 9

William H. Doane, 1875

G D7 G D G
1.Whole - heart - ed thanks - giv - ing to Thee I will bring,
2.Thou, Lord, art a ref - uge for all the op - pressed;
3.Give praise to Je - ho - vah, the might - y deeds tell
4.Be - hold my af - flic - tion, Thy mer - cy ac - cord,
C G A7 D
In praise of Thy mar - vel - ous deeds I will sing;
All trust Thee who know Thee, and trust - ing are blest;
Of Him who has chos - en in Zi - on to dwell,
And back from death's por - tals re - store me, O Lord,
G D7 G D G
In Thee I will joy and ex - ult - ing - ly cry,
For nev - er, O Lord, did Thy mer - cy for - sake
Of Him to whom jus - tice and ven - geance be - long,
That I in the gates of Thy Zi - on may raise
C Am7 C G D G D7 G
Thy Name I will praise, O Je - ho - vah Most High.
The soul that has sought of Thy grace to par - take.
Who vis - its the low - ly and o - ver - throws wrong.
My song of sal - va - tion and show forth Thy praise.

TO GOD BE THE GLORY
11.11.11.11. Ref.

CD # 5 Tracks 21-24

Refrain
D G D
Praise the Lord, praise the Lord, let the earth hear His voice! Praise the
G D7 G D7 G
Lord, praise the Lord, let the peo - ple re - joice! O come to Je - ho - vah, de -
D G C G D D7 G
clare ye His fame, And give Him all hon - or, for just is His Name.

To God Be the Glory

Alternate lyrics by Fanny J. Crosby, 1875

1. To God be the glory, great things He hath done,
So loved He the world that He gave us His Son,
Who yielded His life an atonement for sin,
And opened the Lifegate that all may go in.

Refrain:
Praise the Lord, praise the Lord, Let the earth hear His voice!
Praise the Lord, praise the Lord, Let the people rejoice!
O come to the Father thro' Jesus the Son,
And give Him the glory, great things He hath done.

2. O Perfect redemption, the purchase of blood,
To every believer the promise of God;
The vilest offender who truly believes,
That moment from Jesus a pardon receives.

3: Great things He hath taught us, great things He hath done,
And great our rejoicing thro' Jesus the Son;
But purer, and higher, and greater will be
Our wonder, our transport, when Jesus we see.

Praise God, from Whom All Blessings Flow

TEXT: Thomas Ken, 1637-1711

(Doxology)

From the Genevan Psalter, 1551

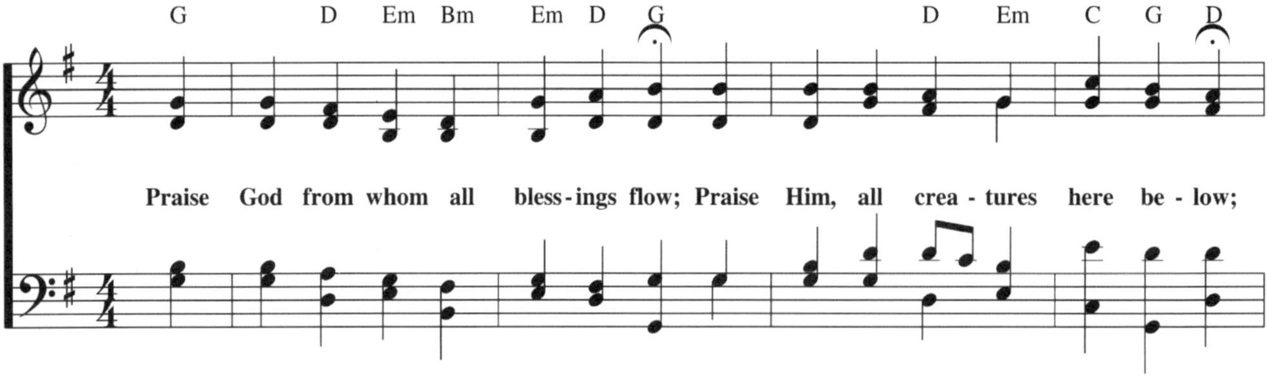
G D Em Bm Em D G D Em C G D
Praise God from whom all bless-ings flow; Praise Him, all crea - tures here be - low;

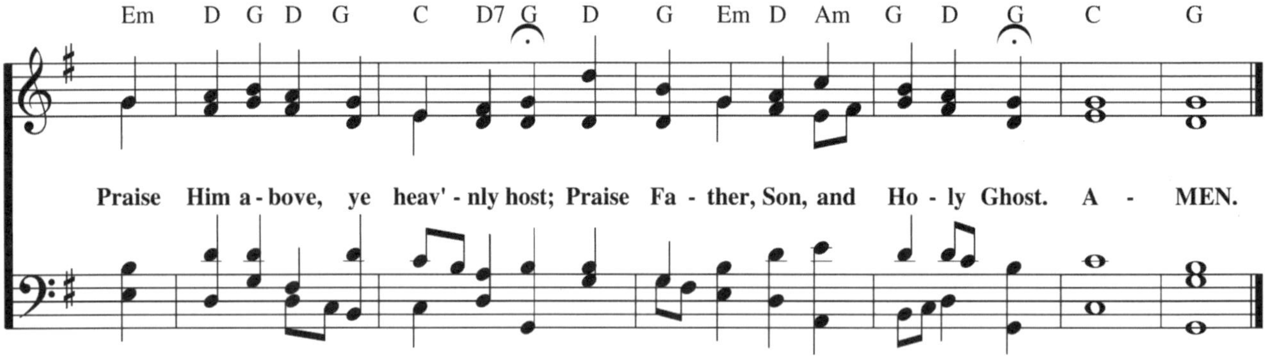
Em D G D G C D7 G D G Em D Am G D G C G
Praise Him a - bove, ye heav' - nly host; Praise Fa - ther, Son, and Ho - ly Ghost. A - MEN.

OLD 100TH
L.. M.

CD # 5 Tracks 25-28